I May Be Wrong,
BUT I DOUBT IT

I May Be Wrong, BUT I DOUBT IT

Mike Royko

HENRY REGNERY COMPANY · Chicago

The author wishes to thank the Chicago Daily News, *where these columns first appeared, for permission to reprint them here.*

First paperback edition published 1971 by Henry Regnery Co.
114 West Illinois Street, Chicago, Illinois 60610

CONTENTS

Police What?

By Popular Demand

THE SOCIAL REGISTER

San-Fran-York on the Lake

It has finally happened, damn it.

A decent, potbellied working man's city is now wearing a turtleneck sweater, long sideburns and a suave look on its face.

And its nose is stuck in a brandy snifter.

The economists and sociologists can explain why it happened. All I know is that it has.

The merchants tell it as well as anyone, with their accounts of the past Christmas season.

Leon Carteaux, Loop jeweler: "It's been different this year. Those who used to shop for costume jewelry wanted something in good gold; those who weren't accustomed to quality were asking to see the better items."

Frank Armanetti, liquors: "They're buying better quality in everything, not worrying about saving 50 or 75 cents on a bottle. We're running short, especially in fine wines."

Dick Innocenti, camera dealer: "Our low-priced cameras didn't sell well. The top of the line sold."

Shelby Young, Allied Radio: "There's been a move toward quality products, more expensive products, on every level of sound equipment."

Siegfried Shattil, art dealer: "This December was the best month we've ever had."

That's the story everywhere. The most expensive pipes, ski equipment, home pool tables, fur rugs, wine racks, men's casual clothing, women's casual clothing and anything else you don't really need. That's what sold.

A town that used to think that six cylinders and a stick shift belonged to a thinking man has put on an imported Irish wool cap and is zipping around in a pseudo-sports car.

It's wearing a razor-cut hair style for six dollars and is gobbling up French food faster than the restaurants can overprice it.

3

Chicago Man has become a dandy right out of the ads. Not long ago, the only distinctive look a Bear fan had was his booze-blurred eyes at the end of the game. Today he dresses out of Abercrombie and Fitch.

Chicago Man might have a well-trimmed beard. He won't drink plain water unless it's on the rocks. Everybody looks like George Hamilton or Norman Ross.

Chicago Woman defies description, with her thighs stylishly bared to 30 mph arctic winds while her torso is wrapped in an artificial Abominable Snowman fur coat.

And it's not just the individual. It's the mood of the city right up (or down, if you prefer) to City Hall. Luxury items have priority over the bread-and-butter projects. Did we really need that $86,000,000 Civic Center more than a few other things?

The city can't get real estate developers even to think about low-cost housing. They want to build top-rent high-rises with carpeting on the balconies and an indoor parking space for EVERY man.

Gracious and stylish living, that's what has Chicago in its grasp. I don't know if my daddy can whip your daddy, but he has a home wine cellar. And my mommy has joined a health club.

It is not a paint-flecked-pants town anymore. The city of the three-flat with flowered wallpaper and linoleum in the parlor, the lunch pail, the shot-and-beer and count-your-change, has become something else: San-Fran-York on the Lake.

Tomorrow is Carl Sandburg's birthday. You remember him. He was named after a high-rise development.

He's dead but he got out of town long before it went to hell in a martini mixer. To observe his birthday, I'm updating his 1916 poem, "Chicago." You know, the one about "Hog Butcher for the World . . . Stormy, husky, brawling . . . City of the Big Shoulders."

Chicago

Hi-Rise for the World
Partygoer, Stacker of Stereo Tapes,
Player with Home Pool Table and the Nation's Jets;
Dapper, slender, filter-tipped,
City of the Big Credit Card:

They tell me you are wicked, and I don't believe them; for
I have seen your painted men tossed in jail every time
they try luring the farm boys.
And they tell me you are crooked, and I answer: Yes,
it is true, but now you steal with the ballpoint pen
and contract, and that's no fun.
And having answered so I turn once more to those who
sneer at this my city, and I join in the sneer and
say to them:
Come and show me another city with razor-cut head
singing so proud to have a Mustang and a white
turtleneck and reservations for dinner.
Fierce as a poodle with tongue lapping for dog yummies.
Wig-headed,
Skiing,
Spending,
Twisting,
Tipping,
Purchasing, discarding, repurchasing,
Under the big restaurant canopy, burgundy sauce
all over his mouth, giggling with white capped teeth.
Under the terrible burden of Consolidated Monthly
Payments, giggling as a disk jockey giggles,
Chuckling even as a smooth salesman chuckles who
has never lost a sale,
Bragging and chuckling that on his wrist is a
battery-operated watch and under his ribs a moroccan
leather belt.

Giggling!
Giggling the silly giggle of the fourth martini
at lunch; half naked, but not sweating, and if
sweating, not offending; Proud to be Hi-Rise
for the World, Partygoer, Stacker of Stereo Tapes,
Player with Home Pool Tables and Jet Handler to the
Nation.

No People Need Apply

The manager of a high-rise building on Lake Shore Drive recently sent this letter to his tenants:

"Dear Tenant:

"We have been receiving numerous complaints on the misuse of the lobbies by adults as well as children.

"We must ask, therefore, that 'Lobby Sitting' be discontinued.

"Please note under Rules and Regulations:

"Children shall not be permitted to loiter or play on the stairways, halls, porches or court areas or in public places generally used by the public or other tenants.

"The sidewalks, entryways, passages, vestibules, halls and stairways outside of the several apartments shall not be used for any other purpose than ingress and egress to and from the respective rooms or apartments.

"We have been asked by many, why we have sofas and chairs in the lobby if we do not permit their use.

"It is the intention of the owners that seating be available for the FEW MINUTES that a guest may be waiting for a tenant, or that a tenant and guest be waiting for a taxi or driver to pick them up, and to enhance our lobby.

"We are sure you will agree that we are constantly extending efforts to maintain our lobbies and public areas in a manner that will be pleasing to you and reflect the prestige of our building. It is our sincere hope that you will co-operate with us."

The letter angered a lady who lives in the building. She said it was directed at the elderly people, who, during the great blizzard, had no place to go. So they sat in the lobby just to get out of their apartments for a few hours.

The lady sent it to me because she felt I would share her anger.

I can't get angry about the letter because I think I understand the feelings of the building manager and the peo-

ple who complained to him about all those old people
hanging around the lobby.

Life just happens to be different in a high-rise than, say,
in a bungalow or three-flat neighborhood.

And High-Rise Man sees things—himself included—in
a different way.

High-Rise Man is like his building—soaring, lean, modern, gracious, cool, handsome, push-button, filter-tipped, a
symbol of today and today's young, calorie-free living.

In the morning, he can leap out of bed and stand there
in his shorts, looking out of his sweeping glass window at
the sun rising over Lake Michigan.

At night, with the lights dimmed, he might stand there
sipping something-on-the-rocks, listening to something
tasteful on his stereo, gazing down at the twinkling lights
on Lake Shore Drive. With a slight smile, he thinks:

"This is It. And I have made It."

Contrast him to Bungalow Man and Three-Flat Man.
We think of ourselves as kind of squat, pot-bellied, ordinary, brick, mortar, sidewalks-by-WPA—just like the real
estate.

The sight of old people is not offensive to Three-Flat
Man and Bungalow Man because even when he is young
he thinks he is getting old.

Besides, old people are part of Three-Flat Man's world.
They're always there, sitting on the front steps, watering
a lawn, watering a dog, taking a walk for the paper, complaining about somebody's punk kids.

But when High-Rise Man and his High-Rise Mate step
out of the cab, nod to the doorman's respectful greeting
and stride through their lobby, it can be jarring—shocking
—to see a bunch of old people sitting around, dozing, knitting, cackling, or even, heaven forbid, coughing.

Not in their lean, young, soaring world.

Children are just as distasteful. When you see a child,
you think of runny noses, scabby knees, diapers, boisterous
behavior—none of which belongs in the world of muted

tones, indirect lighting, thick-rugged hallways and gleaming lobbies.

This is a problem, of course, because old people do live in those buildings. And a few children, too.

And it seems somewhat harsh to bar them from the lobbies entirely.

Possibly the building managers could work out some sort of schedule, as second lieutenants used to do with the day rooms in the service.

They might tell them something like this:

"Dear Tenant:

"It has come to our attention that due to the cold weather some of our elderly tenants would like to leave their apartments and sit in the lobby.

"Therefore, we have amended our rules to permit 'Limited Lobby Sitting.'

"No more than six (6) elderly people will be permitted to sit in the lobby at one time.

"They will space themselves and will use those chairs that are arranged to face AWAY from the main entrance.

"Lobby Sitting will not be permitted during morning hours when tenants are leaving for their offices or during evening hours when dinner guests might be arriving.

"It is NOT allowed on Friday and Saturday nights.

"Lobby Sitting privileges will be revoked, of course, for violations of the above or for repeated complaints of cackling, knitting, dozing, coughing or cracking sounds from joints.

"Regarding children: We suggest that tenants who possess them consider giving them away."

Last of the Big-Time Name Droppers

Those who run the Social Register do it every year. They embarrass some helpless socialite by dropping his name from the book without saying why.

This year it was Borden Stevenson, one of Adlai Stevenson's sons. Last year he was in. This year he is suddenly out. And no explanation was given.

From what I've read about Borden Stevenson, his record seems clean. He hasn't been in jail. He doesn't run around with aldermen. Sure, his brother has gone into politics, but he hasn't been in trouble yet.

Still, the book came out without his name in it. This is probably a tough thing to have to live with. How does Borden Stevenson face his friends at the Cheetah?

Because the Social Register has been committing this injustice for years, I called its New York office to ask why they don't do the right thing and tell a person what he is charged with before he is dropped.

That way, if a socialite is suspected of holding down a regular job or going out with his own wife or staying awake at the opera, he would have a chance to defend himself.

A woman answered the phone at the Social Register office, 381 Park Avenue, New York, and I asked her why Borden Stevenson was dropped.

"I'm sorry. We don't give any information out for publication. None whatsoever. That is one of our laws."

You have your own laws?

"Why, yes."

But isn't it unfair to drop a chap without giving a reason?

"We cannot give reasons. We would hear from them if we gave them out. It is all done on the QT."

How about your editor? Maybe she will tell me.

"I'm sorry but you cannot talk to her. She has often told us never to let anyone talk to her. All we are supposed to say is that nothing may be given out for publication."

Who is your editor?

"That is a secret."

You have a secret editor?

"Yes, everything here is a secret."

Well, who are you?

"You may refer to me, if you wish, as Jane Doe."

That's not your name.

"No, it isn't. My name is also a secret."

Why are you so secretive? You're worse than the FBI.

"I know. Sometimes we joke about that. We even call ourselves 'the FBI.' But we must be up on our toes. People are always snooping around."

Snooping?

"Oh, yes. Reporters like you. That's why it is all hush-hush."

What do they want?

"Oh, they'd love to see our files. That's why our doors are always locked. We don't let people into our office. And the files are kept locked. Why, I've never even seen the files."

What is your job there?

"That is a secret, of course."

Can't you even say how a person gets in the Social Register?

"I can tell you this much—money doesn't matter."

Not at all? A bum can get in?

"What I meant was, social background is what counts."

Does someone just write a letter applying?

"Oh! Ha, ha. No, no! Someone who is already in the register must submit your name and background."

Then you're in.

"Oh, no. Then the advisory committee investigates you and decides."

Who is on the advisory committee?

"That is a secret. To tell the truth, I don't even know who they are. That's how big a secret it is."

Hah! Then how can we really be sure there is an advisory committee?

"Let me assure you, there is."

That's what you say.

"You aren't going to write this up, are you?"

Sure.

"Well!"

So there it is—the socialites who are banished don't even know who banished them.

For all they know, there is no editor and no advisory committee.

My guess is that there's probably just one mummy-like old lady locked in that office, drinking gin and cackling as she crosses out the names of people whose grandfathers didn't ask her to dance at a debutante party in 1902. The old bat.

Move Over, Amy Vanderbilt

As a service to house-party goers, here are some New Year's Eve social tips from well-known social arbiter Slats Grobnik.

They are taken from his best-selling book *My Thirty New Year's Eves Without an Arrest*, which will be published next year or the year after, maybe.

It has been updated to cover current styles and trends.

"*What to Wear:* The current 'in' garments are turtleneck sweaters and 'fun' dresses. Although they were once considered *très* chic, bowling team shirts are 'out.' In selecting a suit (for men) or dress (for women), there is one important consideration to keep in mind: It should be something that can be thrown in the furnace and burned the next day without regrets.

"*What to Drink:* Select one favorite beverage and stay with it all evening. I recommend the always festive boilermaker. (Recipe: Pour one shot of whisky down your throat. Follow with one glass of beer.) Early in the evening, they should be consumed separately. After midnight, however, it is acceptable to combine them in one glass, vase or bowl. Although many people consider it 'in,' I don't recommend drinking from whatever glass happens to be near your arm.

"At midnight, of course, champagne is traditional. But remember—never, never drink it straight from the bottle unless the host does so first. And do not pour it into your beer glass unless the glass is empty. Remember the old saying: 'He who mixes bubbles with booze awakes the next morning still wearing his shoes.'

"*Dining Hints:* Many hostesses will be planning a post-midnight buffet. If you are a guest at such a party, there are just a few things to keep in mind: Before putting the food on your lap, make sure you are seated and that the food is on a plate. Cold chicken, beef sandwiches, olives and pickles can be eaten with the fingers. But do not use your fingers alone while eating Jello-mold salad.

"*Miscellaneous Hints:* If you should feel a bit groggy and think that you might become unconscious, try to find a bedroom in which to collapse. But do NOT select a bed in which the host's children are sleeping or one that is covered with coats and hats. If you should feel a need to rest on the bathroom floor or in the bathtub itself, be courteous and don't lock the door behind you.

"If you need a breath of fresh air, don't lean out of a window, especially if it is higher than the first floor. The practice of throwing objects through, or punching out, windows is 'out' this year. A short walk is the best solution. But while taking a walk, wear a coat. And write down the host's address and pin it to your shirt. Don't lie down on a sidewalk or in a doorway or snowbank; frostbite and gangrene just make the day-after blues more uncomfortable.

"The big moment at any New Year's party is midnight, so you should pace yourself to assure still being awake when it comes. It's customary and proper for the men to kiss the ladies, but you should not kiss the same lady more than three times (unless her husband has passed out, of course), and all kissing should end by 2 A.M., at the latest.

"By all means, try to avoid that social *faux pas* known as the 'crying jag.'

"*When to Leave:* The host and hostess usually give a gentle hint. Watch them. And when the host's head falls back and his eyes roll upward and his breathing comes in gasps, and the hostess is sobbing quietly as she studies her rug and coffee table, it is as good a time as any to slip away."

DARlings on the Move

I've been reading that the Daughters of the American Revolution are trying to change their reputation.

They don't like being thought of as a bunch of funny old conservative ladies, still living in the fife and drum era of their Revolutionary ancestors.

Instead, they want to get in the modern, young swing of things and tackle twentieth-century issues.

The Illinois DAR convention was held this week and I dropped in to see how the face-lifting program was going.

A tiny, white-haired lady was checking credentials outside the Red Lacquer Room of the Palmer House.

"No, no, it is a closed meeting," she said. "You will have to go to the press room and ask them if they will let you in."

Several nice elderly ladies were in the press room, reading *Tribune* editorials.

After offering me a homemade cooky, they got me into the meeting.

About two hundred ladies were scattered about the huge meeting room. All but a handful appeared to be awake. None wore miniskirts. In fact, when they sat down, their skirts fell below the knee.

I whispered to one lady: "Have there been any interesting resolutions passed?"

She told me they had passed a resolution asking the government to promote George Washington to five-star general.

It seems that he never got beyond lieutenant general and this irks the DAR ladies.

"It is a terrible injustice," my seat-neighbor said.

Before she could elaborate, the chairman of the meeting said we should all sing happy birthday to a Mrs. Filtmeyer, which we did.

Then someone whispered in the chairlady's ear and she announced that we should also sing happy birthday to a lady named Jenny, who had played the piano when we sang for Mrs. Filtmeyer.

The singing done, my neighbor told me about other resolutions.

"We passed one praising J. Edgar Hoover as the greatest law enforcement officer in all of history," she said. "He is such a good man.

"And one calling for a more powerful merchant marine. And we resolved to work toward keeping clergymen in the church, and there was one for lower government spending and one opposing metropolitan government.

"And we praised Walt Disney. I'm so sorry about his passing, aren't you?"

Before I could declare my grief, the chairlady introduced the DAR lady who is in charge of putting out a DAR book—*Patriotic Index.*

My neighbor whispered that the book would have the names of patriots of the Revolutionary War.

"Thousands and thousands of names," she said. "Not just soldiers. But people who sewed clothes, cooked and everything. It is the first book of its kind."

Production problems had delayed publication, the speaker revealed.

"Be patient," she said. "I know how eager you are to get your copies. You will like it, very, very much. It will soon be mailed out, so keep your chin up."

Their chins up, the ladies listened to the next speaker, who announced that she was going to tell a joke.

It seems that a lady went to a pet shop to buy a parrot. She asked the owner if it could really talk. The pet shop owner said: "Madam, for $19.50, don't expect Ev Dirksen."

The ladies shook with laughter, among other things, and the meeting galloped on to the highlight of the convention—The March of the Good Citizens.

Several ladies explained it to me:

Schools all over Illinois select students who are Good Citizens to come to the convention. Their parents and teachers also are invited and the DAR makes speeches about how wonderful they are.

"They are waiting outside now," a lady said, in an excited voice. "It is so wonderful to see. They march in so nicely."

The doors were thrown open and Jenny attacked the piano.

First came the fathers, mothers and teachers, trying to march in time to the piano and looking embarrassed.

"It is so wonderful to see fathers walking with their daughters," cried a lady in a purple-feather hat and a turquoise suit.

"Hush," said another lady, who might have been her mother or her daughter.

When the students filed in, a lady hissed at me:

"Make a note of that."

"Of what?" I asked.

"There—a Negro girl. You can see, we aren't segregated. We're living down that business of Marian Anderson not being able to sing in our hall."

"That's right," another lady said. "Any student can come here, if she qualifies on achievement and accomplishment."

And indeed there was a qualified Negro among the dozens of young girls.

While various DAR speakers praised the Good Citizens for their good citizenry, several ladies urged me to remain for lunch. There was to be an exciting luncheon speech by conservative Phyllis Schlafly, author of *A Choice, Not an Echo.*

"She is so, so controversial," a lady said. "Have you heard her?"

I admitted that I had not.

"Oh, you must. I have, and believe me, she can out talk any man."

With that, I fled.

Making It

The Metropolitan Opera peacefully integrated its top-society box seats for last week's opening night.

The evening was the talk of international society because the old, established rich had to give up some of their exclusive box seats to some of the newly rich.

The newly rich got the seats for the first time because they contributed new money to build the new opera house.

Although many of the old rich appeared tense or a bit stiff, there were no reports of violence.

The inside story of the peaceful move-in is told here for the first time.

Much of the credit belongs to the secretly created Metropolitan Opera Human Relations Commission.

It was formed months ago and did hush-hush work behind the scenes, breaking the news to the old, established rich that the newly rich would be sitting with them.

In an exclusive interview, I. Dugood Deeds, the commission's director, explained the agency's role.

"Our job was mainly educational. We had to break down the fears and prejudices of the old rich and keep them from panicking and running to the movies instead of the opera."

Was it a difficult thing to do?

"Not really. Most of the old rich are decent, law-abiding, peace-loving people. But like everyone else, they were afraid. You must remember that many of the old rich have never seen a new rich. They had many false notions."

Such as?

"Well, Mrs. Barry Doe Deeply III was typical. She thought they were all former used-car dealers and would try to sell her something on an easy-payment plan during intermission."

How did you educate them?

"We formed human relations 'teams,' as many suburbs have done, to go have quiet talks with the old rich; to explain that the opera integration is inevitable."

18

The teams were made up of clergymen, I suppose?

"A clergyman, yes. Also a banker, a polo player, a stock-holder, a hairdresser, a tennis instructor and a Hungarian nobleman."

They went door-to-door in the neighborhood?

"No. The old rich don't all live in the same block. Or country. We had to dash around the world a bit."

Where?

"We found Finlay Mustymoney on his yacht in the Mediterranean. When we told him about the planned move-in he was so upset that he threw a cabin boy over the side."

He refused to co-operate?

"At first. But after we assured him that none of the newly rich had a bigger yacht or wanted him to marry their daughters, he was quite reasonable. He even sent a small boat to look for the cabin boy."

Then yacht size was a big objection?

"Not in every case. Some of the old rich feared the presence of the new rich would depreciate their property—such as money."

How?

"Mrs. Vanderocker was particularly upset. She said she didn't trust new money. She thought she would lose the little nest egg her great-great-grandfather, Avaricious P. Vanderocker, worked so hard to set aside when he cornered the world market in food, clothing and medicine."

What did you tell her?

"We showed her some new money. At first she covered her eyes and refused to look at it. She said we were worse than pornography peddlers and threatened to call the DAR. But finally she peeked and was quite surprised to find that it looked just like her money."

That eased her fears?

"Not really. It upset her to know that other money looks like her money. She asked us if FDR caused that, too. But she agreed to the new opera seating when we promised her the newly rich would not wear their money or toss it to people on the main floor."

So most of the fears were economic?

"No. Some were simply afraid the newly rich wouldn't know how to act at an opera. Mrs. Mary Wizely, Jr., thought they would clap too much or act like they were enjoying themselves and embarrass their neighbors. I remember her saying: 'Those people have too much rhythm.' "

She refused to attend?

"No. She was quite agreeable when we told her that the newly rich don't like opera any more than she does."

Your work seems to have paid off. There were no incidents?

"Just one. After the first act, everyone was shouting 'Bravo, Bravo'—except Mr. I. M. Solvent. We had to talk to him."

He was booing?

"No. He was shouting, 'Old power! Old power!' "

Yeah, Mom!

Today's human relations problem, which I will try to solve, is submitted by a Little League mother in the suburb of Bellwood. She writes:

"My son, age eleven, was on a team last year and was literally despised by the man who is manager.

"Why? Because my son passed his son, a year older, in a few activities in the school athletic department.

"He benched my son, called him names, etc., and my son finished up the season with little or no interest left.

"This year we signed him up with the stipulation that he be traded.

"But he was put on the same team, which gave him the alternative of going to the minor league or getting a refund.

"My son is a better than the average baseball player in his age group.

"In fact, a younger son of the manager who is on the team says that if my son goes to the minors, everyone will laugh at him.

"A transfer to the minors would not be our choice. But this man has so much hate built in him and is really seeking revenge. He was probably spited by some adult along the line and is taking it out on the boys.

"The only thing the team learned last year was revenge and hate."

Now, for the solution: It appears this boy is being cheated by his Little League program. The mother says that all he learned in one season was "revenge and hate."

When I was eleven, I did not belong to an organized baseball league. But that year I learned—in addition to revenge and hate—envy, greed, lust and fear.

So it is clear that a change must be made.

But the question is, which way to go: To insist that he be traded? Or to let him go to the minor leagues?

This is one of the most important decisions a mother has to make.

I do not see how she can let him be sent to the minor leagues. A mother does not raise a son, driving him in the station wagon to practice sessions, worrying with him over a sore arm, teaching him the bean ball, only to see him sent to the minors at the age of eleven.

The answer is to demand that the boy be traded.

But the boy must be made to realize that he is being traded for his own good, not because he has failed to make his team.

And that is where a mother's native wisdom must come into play.

If the Bellwood mother handles this properly, the conversation will be something like this:

"Lefty, dear, sit on my lap. Mommy has a surprise for you."

"What, Mom, what?"

"I have decided that you should be traded from the Little Yankees to the Little Giants. We are working out the terms of the swap now."

"But why, Mom?"

"You haven't been used properly at the Yankees. You were riding the bench when you should have been in the ol' starting lineup every day."

"But we don't play every day."

"Every other day, then. But at the Little Giants you will be able to display your strong arm, your blinding speed, your smooth swing, your long-ball potential, your hustle, your all-around baseball savvy and all the other things mommy has taught you."

"Gee, Mom, I appreciate your confidence in me and I promise to put out 100 per cent every game."

"I know, dear. And some day you and I will be proud of you, sitting there with the TV cameras taking your picture as you sign for the biggest bonus in the history of major league baseball."

"How much, Mom? More than five dollars?"

"Never mind, son, that's something mommy and the

lawyer will work out. You just practice throwing the spit-
ter like I showed you."

"OK, Mom."

"And remember our slogan."

"Yeah, Mom, nice kids finish last."

"That reminds me—have you seen your father around?"

"Vogue" on Clout

Many people depend on *Vogue* magazine to tell them what to wear, what to talk about and what—if anything—to think.

If *Vogue* tells them to wear bedpans trimmed in daisies in the Easter Parade, they will run to the nearest medical-supply store to be fitted.

Somebody recently sent me a page from *Vogue* with an item circled. The page claims to contain the "in" things that people are talking about. *Vogue* writes: "People are talking about . . . the rise of the word 'clout.' Among those with 'clout' are President Johnson, the Pope and Ho Chi Minh of Hanoi." (*Vogue* does not want us to confuse him with the Ho Chi Minh of Burlington, Iowa.)

Even for a New York magazine run by a bunch of women this is a surprisingly dumb thing to write. And they have a lot of nerve stealing an old Chicago word and distorting its meaning.

The dictionary definition of clout is, of course, a blow, a shot in the head; to strike something.

But there is also the old Chicago meaning. *Vogue* apparently had that one in mind, but they are confused.

Clout means influence—usually political—with somebody who can do you some good.

A Chicago policeman might have enough "clout" with a ward boss to get a promotion to sergeant. The ward boss might have enough "clout" with the mayor to get his contractor-brother some profitable highway repair work. The mayor might have enough "clout" with the White House to get federal projects and funds for Chicago.

In simple English, a bailiff might say: "Somebody beefed that I was kinky and I almost got viced, but I saw my China-man and he clouted for me at the hall."

As everybody knows, that means: "A citizen complained that I did something dishonest and I was almost fired, but I

contacted my political sponsor and he interceded in my be-
half with my department head."

So, naturally, President Johnson does not have "clout."
He doesn't need it. But somebody else might have "clout"
with him—such as Bobby Baker.

And if the Pope has "clout" with anybody, the matter
should be discussed by theologians, not by *Vogue* writers.

Trying to be helpful, I called *Vogue* in New York. After
clearing through a couple of underlings, I was permitted to
talk to Miss Arlene Talmy, an associate editor who is in
charge of telling us what people are talking about.

I asked her what *Vogue* meant by the item on clout.

She shrieked: "My God! EVerybody knows what it
means!"

(I mentally bet myself that she was wearing a hat and
boots while she worked and that she used to smoke with
a cigaret holder when it was fashionable.)

Maybe everybody you know thinks that the President,
the Pope and Ho Chi Minh (the one in Hanoi) have "clout,"
but I don't know what you mean by it. "Clout" with whom?

"Oh, My God!" she shrieked again. (He had "clout" too?)
"I told you, EV-er-eeee-body is using it EV-er-eeee-where. I
mean, I've seen it in an English paper, in an Italian magazine and, of course, here in New York. Reallllly, it's not that
new."

But what does it mean?

She stopped shrieking. Her voice shifted to the patient
tone one uses with a child, a ninny or a hick newspaperman from Chicago.

"Let me explain it, then, so you will understand."

Please do.

"It means the ability and the means and the power to return a blow when somebody has attacked you."

Does it?

"Of course," she said. "EV-er-eee-body knows that."

You are wrong.

She didn't say anything for a moment. Then she stuttered. Boy, it felt good to make a smart-aleck broad like her stutter. I'll bet nobody has told her she was wrong since she left Iowa, or Nebraska, and went to New York to become a career woman and ruin her complexion.

Before she could start shrieking again, I told her what clout meant and that the word had been stolen from Chicago by New York and was being distorted.

"WELL! That may be what it means in Chicago, but that isn't what it means elsewhere."

She hung up before I could invite her to call me the next time she hears a new "in" word among the "in" people in the ladies' room at *Vogue*.

Take It Off. Take It ALL Off!

Experts say the current semi-nude women's fashions are defeating their own purpose because men are more attracted to fully-clothed women.

The clothing provides "mystery," the experts say, and it is the "mystery" that arouses interest and the slavering beast in men.

Such mystery is lacking in miniskirts and the peek-a-boo fashions.

If this is true—and who would doubt psychiatrists and theologians?—then we can expect some very serious problems in the future.

Fashions swing like a pendulum. This is because most fashion designers are, in the words of a noted psychiatrist, "a bit cracked."

Therefore, in a few years women will probably be more heavily clothed.

And this will lead to more "mystery" than ever before.

I, for one, cringe at the thought of what will happen when men are exposed to the sight of heavily-clothed women.

Newspapers will then be full of stories like these:

• San Francisco (AP)—Police raided four downtown go-go bars Thursday and arrested 22 performers and scores of patrons.

They were the first arrests made under the city's new anti-obscenity ordinance aimed at curbing excesses among go-go performers.

Chief Inspector Roger Dodger said his men took action when they saw the go-go girls dance while wearing mackinaw jackets.

• Chicago (UPI)—Hugh Hefner, publisher of Playboy magazine, defended the current issue against charges of "unparalleled obscenity."

Postal inspectors have seized thousands of copies of the magazine. Their action came after they had received many complaints from church groups, PTA's and other Playboy subscribers.

"There is nothing obscene except in the eye of the beholder," said Hefner, who sought a court injunction forbidding further seizure of his magazines.

The controversy swirled about the November "Playmate of the Month." She is pictured reclining on a bearskin rug while wearing Sears, Roebuck long underwear and Army boots.

• Cannes, France (Reuters)—The Cannes Film Festival was thrown into a near-riot Thursday by the appearance of starlet Rita Neeta.

Police used tear gas to drive off hundreds of youths who converged on Miss Neeta.

The uproar broke out when Miss Neeta stepped from a limousine clad in a complete underwater diving suit.

• Green Bay, Wis. (AP)—In an emergency move, Gov. William Brown canceled Sunday's game between the Packers and the Chicago Bears.

Gov. Brown said the forecast for zero weather threatened a recurrence of last year's disorders when more than 300 men were arrested at the game on charges of molesting women. Most of them said they were thrown into a frenzy by the sight of the bulkily clad women.

• Anchorage, Alaska (UPI)—Officials said Thursday that this city can't accommodate more hippies.

The flower children have poured into Anchorage by the thousands since summer began.

They quickly shed their modest miniskirts and topless bathing suits and donned the new symbol of sexual freedom—the full-length fur Eskimo suit.

• Cicero, Ill. (AP)—Sheriff's police have shut down three syndicate-controlled nightclubs on charges of obscenity.

Sheriff Joseph Woods, who led the raids, said:

"It was the most filthiest, rottenest, dirtiest thing I ever saw. The women came out on the stage wearing nothing but G-strings. Then they slowly got dressed until you couldn't see one inch of flesh."

• Washington (AP)—Evangelist Billy Grammcracker today called for a nationwide "moral uprising against neck-high, ankle-length and wrist-reaching women's clothes."

Grammcracker told a cheering meeting of 55,000 bikini-clad followers:

"Let's return to the decency of our forefathers before everybody in this country turns into a bulky-beast. Take it off—take it all off."

YOU WIN SOME . . .

Sidewalk Slats

The Arlington Heights police are said to have put some kind of ban on the playing of sidewalk hopscotch.

If they are serious, which I doubt, it could not be enforced. It would be a violation of an unwritten common law that says sidewalks belong to kids.

Adults may use them for walking on, plunging to or shoveling off, but, basically, sidewalks are really long, narrow playgrounds.

The best place for a child to play and learn is on a sidewalk. It is his natural environment. If you take a child into the woods, he can fall out of a tree and break a leg and ruin the weekend.

Nobody liked sidewalks more than I did, except Slats Grobnik. To this day, if he walks on grass for more than five minutes, his feet blister. His attitude toward lawns and gardens is summed up when he looks sick and says: "Worms live in that stuff."

When the rest of us would go to Humboldt Park, Slats would shake his head and stay behind, saying: "Anything that can hide behind a fireplug is small enough for me to handle, but how do I know what kind of creep is in the bushes?" He feared being kidnapped and held for ransom because he knew his father didn't believe in touching the savings.

When we built a tree house, Slats wouldn't come up. He said: "If people was meant to live in trees, the squirrels would slip some nuts to the city building-inspector."

So Slats always stayed on the sidewalk and did the things all kids do. And some that nobody had heard of before.

One summer, he spent all of July pitching pennies. He got so good that one Sunday morning he made fourteen straight liners. The precinct captain had that penny bronzed, and it was hung up behind the bar of the corner tavern. Later, Slats's mother put it in with his bronzed baby shoes and his first tooth, a one-inch molar, incidentally.

Naturally, he sold lemonade on the sidewalk. We all did. But Slats was the only one who could sell it when the weather was cold. Even in November he'd have a dozen customers lined up.

One day a plainclothes cop happened to get in line, and that's when they found out that with every glass you got to look at the dirty pictures Slats found in his father's dresser. And that was years before Hugh Hefner came along.

There were days when Slats would just draw or write on the sidewalk with chalk or stones. Mostly dirty words. Then he'd hide in a gangway and peek out to see if ladies were offended. If they were, he'd go "hee-hee." Slats would have been a natural hippie.

Sometimes he'd spend the day just lying on the sidewalk, face down, forehead pressed against the pavement, not moving a muscle. He'd be watching the ants in the crack. People from outside the neighborhood were startled, especially when he'd hiss: "Boy, they're murdering each other."

Once a drunk came out of the tavern and tripped over him. Slats pretended to have a broken rib and the drunk gave him five dollars to keep quiet. Slats moaned louder and he got five dollars more. For a long time after that, Slats thought about going to law school.

Even when he didn't feel like doing anything, Slats did it on the sidewalk. He liked to lean against a wall and spit. That wasn't as disgusting as it sounds, although it was pretty disgusting.

He'd just stand there, not moving or saying anything, and every two or three minutes he'd go "phttt" between his two front teeth. He'd keep it up all day, quitting only when he felt weak from dehydration.

A big event for Slats was when a new section of sidewalk was put down. He'd sneak out at night, take off his shoe and put his footprint in it.

His feet are hard to describe. They were very big and shaped kind of funny. So people got nervous when they saw the print. But a man from a museum came out and said there was nothing to worry about because whatever made the print had been dead for millions of years.

What Slats was best at was walking on a sidewalk without stepping on lines. We all did that for good luck when we happened to be walking, but Slats would go walking for hours just to avoid stepping on lines.

One day he decided to try for a world's record, and he left without telling anybody. He was gone for three days, walking all over the city, avoiding stepping on lines.

When he got back home he yelled: "Don't worry, ma, I wasn't kidnapped."

His father waved the bank book and triumphantly said: "See, I was right. There was no reason to disturb the savings."

The Hustler

Ralph knows a good deal when he sees one. That's how he has avoided getting involved in bad deals, such as regular work.

He doesn't need the biggest profit in the world. Far from it. When things are going good, he lives at the YMCA. When they aren't too good, he lives in Clark Street fleabags.

But he doesn't drink, smoke or, at sixty, run around with women. He has a small income from an inheritance, so a few dollars a day extra is all he needs for comfort.

Ralph ran into one of the best deals he ever saw this summer. He was going past a religious bookstore when he saw some paperback Bibles for only 25 cents. Ralph went in and bought a small stack.

It's not that he's religious. He isn't. "I used to have a religion that I was raised in. But they had me brainwashed and I got out of it. I'm a philosopher, see. I believe in not getting tangled up in organized society. And I believe in brotherhood, compassion and love."

Full of brotherhood and love, Ralph went over to Randolph Street and started getting his investment back. He stopped people outside the Sherman House, saying: "Hello, brother. How are you! I'd like you to see the message for you that there is in this book. I'd like you to have this. . . ."

When a nice old man calls you brother and slaps a Bible in your hand, you can't toss it back at him or make a scene. You might even stick something in his mitt. Frank got from 50 cents to a dollar for each of the books and he got rid of them in a few minutes.

The next day he was back for another stack. They went just as fast. He changed locations every day, working the airport and around different downtown hotels and cab stands. He even sold some to cab drivers, which is a pretty good trick.

"I am a high-pressure salesman," Ralph says. "But I don't like to work hard at it. I guess there is no limit how many of these I could get rid of in a day but there is no point in overdoing something."

A week ago, Frank went in to get his supply, but instead he found himself facing the very large Rev. William Maloney, pastor of the Loop's Christ the King Lutheran Church and manager of the King's Corner store on Jackson.

"I happened to see you on Randolph Street selling them," said Mr. Maloney, who has a gentle voice but is well over six feet high and wide in the shoulders.

Ralph forgot his love of humanity.

"You call yourself a minister? You are nothing but a detective, sneaking around and spying on me."

The minister patiently explained that the paperbacks cost 60 cents to print and are sold for a quarter because the church wants people to have them. If the nonprofit organization that prints the Bibles knew they were being resold for profit, they might be upset. (Paperback pornographers never cut their prices: a sign of the times.)

A good deal was blowing up on him, so Ralph was not interested in words, words. He shouted, so Mr. Maloney tried to steer him outside.

"You big John Wayne, you. Don't try to use your totalitarian methods on me. I warn you." Then Ralph beat it. But the vendetta had begun.

"I was born and raised around Taylor and Halsted, where the Sicilians lived," said Ralph, in a tone that indicated he would not let the insult pass. And he has not.

The next day the store was quiet, the customers were browsing. The door flew open and Ralph leaped in, his finger pointing at Mr. Maloney, his jaw flapping and the words gushing out.

"You devil . . . you detective . . . you John Wayne. . . ." He darted around for a few moments, then he was gone.

That's the way it is now for Mr. Maloney. At any moment of the day, Ralph might hop in and call him a John Wayne.

"I tried to explain to him about the prices," the minister says. "But he's pretty hot-tempered."

Meanwhile, Ralph is not giving up on the Bible business, despite his new responsibility of running a feud.

"I can get more. If I was a bad guy, I could write to a Bible outfit in New York and tell them I want them for friends. I'd get them free. But I wouldn't do that.

"It so happens I know other places here I can get them for 30 or 35 cents. So I don't need those two-bit copies, especially from that John Wayne character."

Destiny's Tot

Frank Diaz is in trouble with the police again. This time they say he was picking out a pair of shoes in a store at Milwaukee and Armitage—at two o'clock in the morning.

Once again, Frank says it is a bum rap. To hear him tell it, the police have a special unit that does nothing but dream up bum raps for Frank.

The last time was when the traffic man put a ticket on Frank's car, which was parked illegally on Division Street, where Frank lives. Some of Frank's friends didn't think Frank should have a ticket so they busted up the squad car. Frank got off, though, because he said he was sleeping when it all happened and couldn't have thrown a rock through the squad car window.

That's the way it is with Frank. He says the police department even deprived him of his high school education because they caught him riding in a stolen car when he was just a kid. "I was only a passenger," Frank says.

And now the shoes. Once again Frank has an explanation:

"Tell me, what do you think—you think I would do somethin' like that? Me? A 22-year-old man, I'm goin' to snatch shoes from a window? A man with a wife and two children? Why should I go around snatchin' shoes?"

That is a good question. Frank is built like a fullback and would look foolish snatching anything smaller than a safe.

"The way things happened, see, was like this. It was Saturday night, see, and I got all dressed up in my suit and everythin', you know, and I was over to a dance on Ashland and Van Buren in a hall over there."

Even a 22-year-old man with a wife and two children has got to get out and unwind once in a while.

"So when the dance was over, I was takin' one of my buddies home in a car. And I come around the corner, over

39

there around Milwaukee and Armitage, and I bump into this other car, see?

"Four guys jump out of the other car and they grab my buddy. So I took off.

"I run around the block and I'm comin' back to see what happened to my buddy. Then I hear these shots."

That's the way it is with Frank. One minute he's minding his own business, driving a buddy home from a dance. The next minute he's escaped the clutches of four hoods and the air is ringing with gunfire.

"I hear those shots and I think maybe it's the gang comin' again, so I take off runnin' again, see? I run into an alley. Then I get hit on the head."

Who hit you?

"I dunno. I'm on the ground and I see a cop standin' over me and I remember his voice comin' through my conscious. He says I snatched some shoes from a store window and he says he seen me do it."

That's the way it is with Frank. One minute he's minding his own business, driving a buddy home from a dance. Then suddenly he has escaped the clutches of four hoods, the air is ringing with gunfire and Frank is flat on his back in an alley, accused of stealing shoes.

"So they took me to court and the judge says my bond is $10,000. Now ain't that somethin'? Burglars, murderers and thieves, they get $10,000 bond. But I'm just charged with stealin' shoes.

"But my brother Frank Diaz made bond for me. You remember him. He got the same name as me—Frank Diaz. He's the older Frank Diaz and I'm the younger Frank Diaz.

"I get a continuance so I can get a lawyer and prove I'm innocent of stealin' shoes. But I don't know if I can do it."

The problem is simple. Your buddy can be a witness that you were just coming home from a dance.

"Nah, I don't know his name. I just met him that night."

Where does he live? You were taking him home.

"I dunno. He was going to tell me when we got there."

That's the way it is with Frank. One minute he's driving a buddy home. Suddenly he escapes the clutches of four hoods, the air is filled with gunfire, Frank is charged with stealing shoes, and his buddy vanishes and Frank doesn't know his name.

"I don't know why things are always happenin' to me," Frank says.

Just plain bad luck, I say.

Vince, a Soldier's Soldier

On these holidays I always remember Vince. He was one of my old comrades-in-arms.

He wasn't a fallen comrade. None of mine was. The only way they fell was off a stool.

Before enlisting, Vince had been a gambler in Montreal. He was older than most of us and didn't have to join. But he came across the border and joined because some gambling enemies were after him in Montreal.

He was an expert in poker, blackjack, dice, bribery of sergeants and forging of passes, and he knew more about diseases than the medics or even the chaplain. We considered him a natural leader.

There's someone like Vince in every outfit of every branch of the service. He never had to do anything. He never cleaned a latrine or picked up a cigaret butt. He never scrubbed a floor. Most of his time was spent in his bunk, just goofing off.

Just doing nothing and getting away with it is a wonderful feeling in the service. It's less of a luxury in civilian life, of course, because union contracts guarantee it.

He was always getting in trouble, going AWOL and spending a few days in the stockade and such, but he turned that to his advantage. We were all learning to be radio operators. But Vince, with stockade interruptions, wasn't making a "dit." At the rate he was going, he figured the Korean War would have to end long before he mastered "dit-dit."

The only part of military life that disturbed Vince was the daily routine of marching to school.

It infuriated him because it meant getting into semi-dress uniform and marching about a mile in the blazing Mississippi sun.

All the troops marched past the general's office and the general would come out and stand in the shade on a reviewing stand and return our salutes and eyes-right and that stuff.

Vince said the only reason we had to march to school in semi-dress uniform, instead of shuffling there in fatigues, was that the general got his kicks from being saluted.

So while most of us were satisfied to loathe second lieutenants, Vince developed a hatred for the general. He thought bigger than we did in everything.

One night he put down his cards, which saved us all a few dollars, and told us he had thought of a way to get the general.

There was to be a Base Queen Contest in a week or so. The wives and girlfriends of the men in the various training schools were eligible. It was the sort of thing some goof of a recreation officer thought up in hopes of keeping people out of the off-limits bars for a few hours.

The queen would get a trophy and would be congratulated by the general. Pictures would be taken, probably of the queen giving the general a kiss. The pictures would go to the local newspapers and the base paper.

Vince took a picture of a girl out of his footlocker and asked us what we thought her chances were.

Had she been moderately ugly, her chances would have been good, considering the pictures hanging above most of the bunks.

As it was, she was stunning. She was the best-looking girl any of us had ever seen, and we all said obscene things to show our admiration.

We asked who she was.

Vince said she was a girl he knew back in Montreal and that her profession was the world's oldest. As a gambler, he had known some interesting people.

Vince's idea was that we would all chip in and he would fly to Montreal and bring her back to the nearby town. It could be done in a weekend. And out of affection for him and for a small profit, she would be happy to make the trip.

Then she would enter the queen contest as Vince's fi-
ancée, and most likely win.

Once the picture of her holding her trophy and smooching with the general was in all the local papers and in the
military paper, it would be mailed to the vice cops in Montreal, who knew the girl, and the police-beat reporters on
the Montreal papers, who knew the story.

Soon it would be flashed across the country by the news
services.

Vince said he was confident the publicity would embarrass the general and raise the morale of the troops. We
called Vince dirty names to show how much we admired his
genius.

Someone asked Vince if he wasn't afraid the stunt would
get him a court-martial. He said he'd take an oath that he
thought she worked the night shift in a factory.

We got a bankroll together. Vince bought a three-day
pass and left.

I got a letter from him three weeks later, after a skinny-
legged USO volunteer got to be queen.

He said his enemies weren't around Montreal anymore,
so he was resigning from the service, at least until they
came and got him. He said he had looked the girl up anyway and that she was still beautiful. He didn't mention the
money. But he said I could have his deck of cards and told
me how they were marked.

I was in Montreal a few years ago and I looked in the
phone book. He was there. I took out a dime, then put it
back. If it turned out he was married, bald and selling insurance, I'd rather not know.

Meet Number One

No cheering crowd of fans greeted Al Carter at O'Hare Airport. The mayor didn't lead a parade on State Street when Al came home, bringing glory to Chicago.

The City Council didn't even pass a resolution praising him in lofty language aldermen don't understand.

But Al has learned not to expect praise for his deeds. He is one of the city's few genuine champions but hardly anyone knows about him.

Carter, a dance-band drummer by trade, devotes much of his energies to roaming North America, looking for lines to be first in.

Chances are you've seen a picture of him or read a little story about one of his firsts.

He has been the first motorist on new expressways. He was first to enter the fairs in New York and Seattle, the first across many new bridges, into new buildings, at sporting events.

He recently had his biggest challenge—Expo 67 in Montreal.

Here, in an exclusive interview I obtained by being awake when Carter dropped in, is his story:

"I began planning three years ago. You remember when you asked me what new horizons I would cross, and I said I was retiring from getting firsts? Well, I was already planning this. Naturally, I had to keep it a secret. Others had the same idea and I wanted to lull them into a false sense of security, the fools.

"I began writing to officials in Montreal, ordering the first ticket. I got it. But that was only half the battle. The big thing is to be first through the gates.

"I knew I'd have stiff competition. The toughest would be two guys from New York—an uncle and his nephew. They're pretty good and I've run into them several times.

"They were aiming for Expo 67 and I knew it because of

45

what happened at the New York Fair in '64. I beat them out in their own home town, by a matter of minutes.

"I remember how they looked at me. Like this. . . ."

Carter demonstrated a steely-eyed, grim, threatening look.

"They told me: 'We shall meet again.'

"Well, I got to the gate at Expo 67 just twenty-four hours before the gates were to open. Why twenty-four hours? I've got a formula but I can't reveal it. It includes weather, the event, the size of the event, the airline schedules, a lot of things. But twenty-four hours was my estimate.

"It was perfect. A couple of hours later the guys from New York showed up. Or I think they did. They stopped a long distance away when they saw me. And they turned around and left. They couldn't face me. They couldn't take being second again. Do you blame them?

"Then the others showed up. But they were all too late. They're always too late. You got it or you ain't got it. They don't have it.

"When they see me, they always leave. What's there to being second?

"It was a long cold night. How did I spend it? I'll tell you something that I've never revealed before.

"I've always had this question in my mind, whether there are really super-intelligent beings in space. You know, in flying saucers.

"So when I'm alone on a new expressway, or on a bridge, or at a fair gate, I sometimes stand up and say:

" 'Helllooooo, super-intelligent beings in space. I will not harm you. Do you have a message for us earthlings? Place your trust in me. I will deliver the message. Contact me. Give me your message. There's nobody watchin'.'

"I'm convinced that there's nobody up there because I've never had an answer, except once from a bum I didn't notice sleeping under a tree, and he just jumped up and yelled and ran away.

"Anyway, morning came and I was first through the

gate. They grabbed me and brought me to the reporters for a press conference. There were more than 100 of them there, all interviewing me. Isn't that nuts? I interrupted the *New York Times* a couple of times in order to answer a question from the Associated Press. That felt good because I'm feuding with the *New York Times* for not giving me credit at the New York Fair for being first. They cut me out of their story because they hate to give Chicago credit for anything.

"Then a guy from the Canadian Broadcasting Company got me on the air. I asked him if it was going all over Canada. He told me it was being heard by 800,000,000 people around the world via satellite. I said: 'I didn't know there was that many.'

"And that's how I did it. You now have the full story. I don't want anything for it, except maybe that you mention that I am always available to work with jazz groups, at rodeos and dances, and I recently worked the drums at 'An Evening with Franklyn MacCormack' at the Civic Opera. That was in Wayne King's orchestra.

"And I'm all done with firsts. Expo 67 was my final accomplishment. Now I'm going into retirement."

We shook hands and he left. At the elevator, he neatly shouldered between four people, hopped on first and punched the button for One.

La Salle Street Lament

Everybody on La Salle Street was talking about what happened. Maishe Baer has gone away.

Maishe was one of the most famous men on the street. He ran the H & H Restaurant, 208 N. La Salle, a favorite hangout for City Hall pols, judges, clerks, lawyers and fixers from Traffic Court, car hikers and reporters, bondsmen and secretaries, policemen and that breed of hoodlums who wear golf slacks and alpaca sweaters at noon on a workday.

It is sort of a lunchroom-style Fritzel's, specializing in blintzes, corned beef and potato pancakes.

The customers all knew Maishe. He sat behind the cashier's counter, a fat, glowering man, always whispering into a telephone or grunting when someone said hello.

Wednesday he wasn't there. The place was gloomy.

Mike Brodkin, one of the city's leading lawyers for hoodlums, sat in Booth One near the cashier's desk, nervously chewing dark bread, whispering about Maishe to Maishe's friends and jumping up to use the phone behind the cashier's counter, a special privilege for big shots at the H & H.

Someone said to a waitress: "It is really tragic." She almost wept into a bowl of cold borsch with sour cream.

It was just before lunch that Maishe went away. He kissed his wife good-by and told her to be brave and not to worry.

Then, holding a paper over his face so his picture couldn't be taken, he marched away to jail.

Maishe, the famous restaurant man, was one of the 13 hoods who were found guilty of stealing about a million dollars' worth of silver alloy and camera equipment in four separate highway truck heists.

That surprised everybody. Nobody ever thought that Maishe, at the age of 52, was the kind of guy to get involved in something like armed highjacking of interstate shipments.

It is true, of course, that Maishe has always been a controversial figure. The controversy was over what Maishe's racket really was.

Some said he was a juice man. He once got a nice newspaper writeup when a man complained that when he got behind in his juice payments, Maishe speeded him up by poking him with lit cigarets.

Others said he was a muscle guy. The police tell a story about a barber-bookie in the Loop who forgot to turn in all of the bets to those upstairs. Maishe talked to him about it so much that the barber's leg broke.

Still others said he was a bookie himself. They got this idea because sometimes Maishe's two phones behind the cashier's desk were always ringing.

There are those who thought he was a fixer. That's what a police sergeant in Traffic Court thought when Maishe shoved a $100 bill at him before one of Maishe's friends came to trial.

But Maishe's real admirers said he was just an old-fashioned, all-around talent from the West Side, a follower of Lenny Patrick, one of the top Jewish hoodlums in the syndicate.

Maishe, to his credit, told a wonderful story in federal court about how he was an innocent victim of crazy circumstances and didn't have anything to do with hijacking. The jurors couldn't find it in their hearts to believe him.

Nobody accused Maishe of actually going out on a U.S. highway and pointing a gun at truck drivers coming out of truck stops.

Maishe was accused of being one of the men who helped get rid of the hot merchandise. The FBI said he took a truck loaded with camera equipment and stashed it in a downtown garage, right near his restaurant.

But Maishe told it a different way. He said a man named Pat Schang caused him all the trouble. All he knew about Schang was that he used to come into the restaurant with lawyers. "We have a million lawyers a day come in duh restaurant."

One day Pat Schang called and said he had a truck that broke down on a highway and he wanted to tow it to a downtown garage. Did Maishe know of a garage? Sure. Maishe parked his car in one all the time. So he told the garage, they said OK, Schang brought the truck there and that's all he knew about any trucks.

"Then I went to the Dearborn Club," Maishe told the jurors, "for some steam and sun."

Then one day at dawn, many months later, "The FBI knocked on my door. They said: 'You are under arrest . . . for bringing a load of film in the garage at 120 W. Lake.' I said: 'You must be silly. I never brought no film over there.' "

And the FBI agents stood there that morning, Maishe said, and watched him put on his pants and socks to go downtown.

The jury wasn't even impressed when Maishe told them how coolly he had treated Schang on another occasion.

"Schang said: 'Listen, can you do me a favor?'

"I said: 'What is the favor?'

"He said: 'I want you to give an alibi that I was in this restaurant in September when a bank was stuck up in one of the suburbs.'

"I said: 'Are you crazy? What do I remember about September? How can I say you were in my restaurant? I don't lie for you or anybody else.'

"He went out of there mad. I never seen him no more."

Maishe even told the jury about how tough it was for him when he was a kid: "Eighth grade . . . I never went to school."

His lawyer told how hard Maishe works. When he's not in the restaurant, he is out peddling watermelon in the summer, or Christmas trees in the winter.

And Maishe even talked about his mother and revealed that his name isn't really Maishe Baer. That's just what people downtown call him. To his neighbors in Lincolnwood, he is Morris Saletko.

"Maishe Baer . . . I had dat name when I was a baby. My mother gave me dat name."

The jury just wouldn't buy Maishe's story. So now he has to wait a couple of weeks for the judge to decide if Maishe will get 15 years or what. It could be worse. Some of the 13 might get life for kidnapping the truck drivers. And a couple of others in the gang talked too much before the trial and were found very dead from such ailments as ice picks.

The only thing that made the gang happy was that Potatoes Daddano, a real syndicate big shot, was found not guilty. That's always the way.

It probably didn't make Maishe feel very good, though, that a fellow La Salle Street figure pronounced him guilty.

The foreman of the jury was a vice-president of the First National Bank. But, then, he probably never eats in the H & H and didn't know he was messing around with Maishe Baer.

The Balloon Man

John C. McCormick was buried yesterday. Some of his friends suggested that something be written because his death was a loss to the city.

Mr. McCormick, who was 77, was in the balloon business. This meant that on Saturdays and Sundays he walked around the street selling balloons to kids.

There aren't many balloon men left. Those who still sell balloons usually work the parks, carnivals, baseball games and other public events. Few of them just walk around a neighborhood.

McCormick usually worked the Italian section, around Taylor and Halsted, or the Bridgeport neighborhood. He said he enjoyed those neighborhoods because the people and children had changed less than in most other places. The sight of a balloon man could still make a child's eyes widen in those neighborhoods.

McCormick hadn't always sold balloons. His real profession, earlier in life, had been running a flea circus. He got into that line when he ran away from home at the age of twelve and joined a circus. He never told anyone where his home had been.

After a few years as a circus roustabout, he learned the flea business and became an attraction. His wife sold the tickets and he put the fleas through their routine.

There aren't many flea circuses going today. McCormick said he felt they were killed off by television, which provides the same level of entertainment except that it uses people instead of fleas.

When his wife died about twenty years ago, McCormick let the fleas go and just drifted around, riding freight trains most of the way. He had no family, not even distant relatives, so he was able to finally settle on the W. Madison Skid Row without having to worry about embarrassing someone.

It isn't a bad place to live, in some ways. There are a

couple of hotels that are clean and quiet. They cater to sober elderly men living on small pensions who enjoy each other's company and don't want to be troubled by call girls, pandering bellhops, jewel thieves, noisy drunks, bookies and other types found in the better downtown hotels.

McCormick went there because he didn't have much money. You don't build much of a pension fund operating a flea circus. That's when he turned to selling balloons.

He liked it because it was an outdoor job. He had never worked in an office or factory. The trouble was, he wasn't a very good businessman. He managed to lose money selling balloons.

He charged enough for them. But he could not stand to see a child without money look enviously at his friends. So he gave away as many balloons as he sold.

In order to keep his balloon business running he had to take another job, cleaning up the cafeteria in old St. Patrick's Church and school, Adams and Desplaines. They gave him meals and a few dollars a day, which helped him buy more balloons.

The only time he missed a summer weekend on Taylor Street or Loomis Street was when he suffered a stroke. But he always bounced back, even when he collapsed on Madison and the cops thought he was just drunk and tossed him in a cell.

His friends at the church say they'll probably be able to find someone to replace him in the cafeteria-cleaning job. But they doubt if anyone will be willing to take over his balloon territory.

IF YOU'RE BLACK, STAY BACK

Millions in His Firing Squad

FBI agents are looking for the man who pulled the trigger and surely they will find him.

But it doesn't matter if they do or they don't. They can't catch everybody, and Martin Luther King was executed by a firing squad that numbered in the millions.

They took part, from all over the country, pouring words of hate into the ear of the assassin.

The man with the gun did what he was told. Millions of bigots, subtle and obvious, put it in his hand and assured him he was doing the right thing.

It would be easy to point at the Southern redneck and say he did it. But what of the Northern disk-jockey-turned-commentator, with his slippery words of hate every morning?

What about the Northern mayor who steps all over every poverty program advancement, thinking only of political expediency, until riots fester, whites react with more hate and the gap between races grows bigger?

Toss in the congressman with the stupid arguments against busing. And the pathetic women who turn out with eggs in their hands to throw at children.

Let us not forget the law-and-order type politicians who are in favor of arresting all the Negro prostitutes in the vice districts. When you ask them to vote for laws that would eliminate some of the causes of prostitution, they babble like the boobs they are.

Throw in a Steve Telow or two: the Eastern and Southern European immigrant or his kid who seems to be convinced that in forty or fifty years he built this country. There was nothing here until he arrived, you see, so that gives him the right to pitch rocks when Martin Luther King walks down the street in his neighborhood.

They all took their place in King's firing squad.

And behind them were the subtle ones, those who never

say anything bad but just nod when the bigot throws out his strong opinions.

He is actually the worst, the nodder is, because sometimes he believes differently but he says nothing. He doesn't want to cause trouble. For Pete's sake, don't cause trouble!

So when his brother-in-law or his card-playing buddy from across the alley spews out the racial filth, he nods.

Give some credit to the most subtle of the subtle. That distinction belongs to the FBI, now looking for King's killer.

That agency took part in a mudslinging campaign against him that to this day demands an investigation.

The bullet that hit King came from all directions. Every two-bit politician or incompetent editorial writer found in him, not themselves, the cause of our racial problems.

It was almost ludicrous. The man came on the American scene preaching nonviolence from the first day he sat at the wrong end of a bus. He preached it in the North and was hit with rocks. He talked it the day he was murdered.

Hypocrites all over this country would kneel every Sunday morning and mouth messages to Jesus Christ. Then they would come out and tell each other, after reading the papers, that somebody should string up King, who was living Christianity like few Americans ever have.

Maybe it was the simplicity of his goal that confused people or the way he dramatized it.

He wanted only that black Americans have their constitutional rights, that they get an equal shot at this country's benefits, the same thing we give to the last guy who jumped off the boat.

So we killed him. Just as we killed Abraham Lincoln and John F. Kennedy. No other country kills so many of its best people.

Last Sunday night the President said he was quitting after this term. He said this country is so filled with hate it might help if he got out. Four days later we killed a Nobel Peace Prize winner.

We have pointed a gun at our own head and we are squeezing the trigger. And nobody we elect is going to help us. It is our head and our finger.

Just Another Riot

It was almost ten o'clock Saturday night. That's when the casual crowd, the slacks-and-sweater crowd, stops in the place for a bite.

They come from the movies for a pizza. Or they step out for some martinis and a butt steak. It's a comfortable place for when they don't want to dress up but want good food and drinks.

And it's the kind of neighborhood, Far Northwest, where people don't worry about the food budget if they drop an extra ten or fifteen dollars. Not rich, but comfortable. The kids have cars.

A color TV flickered at the end of the padded bar and somebody on the screen was screaming and running from door to door on an empty street. A killer was after him and tough Mannix wasn't there to help.

The chatter faded for a moment. Nobody knew the plot or why he might get killed, but it was good terror in itself. He screamed and ran, Mannix didn't show, the killer squeezed the trigger, the man twitched, spun and died.

"Waitress, another martin with a twist, please. Make it two."

A man in a turtleneck came in and took a stool at the bar. The stools have padded backs on them and they swivel.

"What do you hear?" he asked, thumbing at the TV.

"Nothing yet," the bartender said, "but I hear it's bad. Daley called in the Army."

It was bad, ten or twelve miles away. That's where the flames were eating a hole in the ghetto, where people were shouting at each other, where the hospital emergency rooms were overflowing. It was so bad that there were more troops in Chicago than at Khe Sanh.

But that restaurant-bar with its regular Saturday night crowd was a more important place than Madison, 63rd Street or the Cabrini Homes.

What was said and felt and thought in that bar was more

60

important than what was said and felt and thought on the fifth floor of City Hall, where the mayor was losing weight fast.

What the people in the bar said was more significant than what the ministers in the churches would say the next morning.

If there was a glimmer of hope, it would have to show here. These were the people who would decide which way society would go.

They had said it themselves, probably, when they talked about open housing, busing, all the other things that were entwined in the distant fury. They had said that you can't legislate what's in a man's heart, right? Right, they answered themselves.

There would have to be some understanding here, a new outlook, if America was to change direction. That's what everybody in high position was saying, anyway.

And they are right. This was a neighborhood where two congressional candidates fought it out on one issue: Which one was more opposed to Negroes' coming in. This is where only two members of a PTA talked up for busing.

The people here didn't like King when he marched and sang. But now he was dead. And they HAD worried about Mannix's friend.

Mannix avenged his friend, and the TV slid into the news. There was only one story.

Looting was shown. A couple of black kids walked out of a store carrying things.

A young man at a table loudly said: "They ought to kill 'em. Right there, kill 'em." The young man's lady, a pretty, soft-eyed blond, nodded. Had their sense of justice been stirred that violently by slum rats, lynchings or Mrs. Liuzzo?

A tall man stared at the screen while slowly chewing his sandwich. The waitress watched his table closely because the man's name is Harry and he is one of the city's best-known Democratic politicians. He used to run a huge federal agency here and now he holds an elective office.

The screen showed some black people who had lost their homes in the flames. One of the people at Harry's table, a woman, said: "That's a shame. They save a down payment then that happens."

Harry's face twisted. "Down payment!" he scoffed. "They haven't reached that level yet."

He never talked that way when he was rooting around for the black vote. But this was his neighborhood and you can relax in your own neighborhood.

The TV brought Martin Luther King into the room. Old film clips. He was preaching against violence. Somebody called out: "Waitress, another martin, huh? With a twist, no olive."

A couple got up to leave. The man stretched and patted his tummy. As he walked to the door with a roll he glanced back at the TV. King was exhorting his audience to be peaceful. "They should've killed him then," the stomach-patter said. His quip drew chuckles from several tables and he giggled at his own words.

Somebody at the bar said: "Hey, for chrissakes, enough is enough, huh?" The bartender turned the knob. King left. A comedian appeared. There were grunts of appreciation and the conversation lifted. Laughter returned.

Whatever they disliked about him alive, they disliked about him dead. And all that had happened this weekend was that there was another riot. Bigger, maybe, but just another riot. Another martin, please, with a twist, no olive.

The Welcome Wagon Didn't Come

Buying a house is risky business. Just ask Alice and Charlie Roberts.

About five months ago they went house hunting because their neighborhood was getting too tough and they wanted a house of their own. Part of the American dream.

A real estate man took them to the Southwest Side, to a neighborhood of winding streets, big back yards, two-story brick houses, trees, grass.

The house was empty because the former owner had lost it to a VA foreclosure. It looked like a good buy, $19,500, six rooms.

The Roberts looked at the local school and saw white and Negro kids. That was OK because they didn't mind an integrated neighborhood.

They closed the deal and moved in. Now, five months later, Mrs. Roberts wishes she had never seen the place.

There's nothing wrong with the house. It's the neighborhood that bothers Mrs. Roberts.

What she and Charlie didn't know about the neighborhood was that it is not integrated; it is all white, but the Roberts are Negroes. The school fooled them. The Negro children they saw are bused in.

If they had known that, Mrs. Roberts said, they would have gone straight back to 63rd and Blackstone, the Rangers and all.

That way she wouldn't be spending her days cooped up in a house with the drapes always closed and the children seldom outside; and her nights waiting for bricks to again crash through the windows or the garage to again burn.

She can laugh now, though, when she recalls her surprise on moving day. "When we got here, there were already a couple of police cars outside and people all outside their houses. A lady was screaming for us to stay off her lawn. In December, can you imagine? I told Charlie, 'Let's go back.' But we had bought it so we moved in."

A few nights later the first brick came through the picture window and a police car was stationed outside. Then a rock came through the back window. Later, during the blizzard, someone poured gasoline on the garage and tried to set it afire.

And all the while, there was The Sign, which read: NEXT HOUSE.

It is on the front porch of the house next door, directing prowlers with rocks or gasoline to the right house.

The sign was put up by John J. Bowden, a gaunt undertaker who works for the Egan Funeral Home, 3700 W. 63rd Street.

Bowden says he put up the sign because he feared someone might make a mistake and throw a brick through his window. "It is self-protection," said Bowden, who has ignored pleas of police and city officials to take it down.

The sign is a symbol of the neighborliness that has greeted the Roberts.

They were in the house one day when several men came in and said they wanted to buy the house, warning of the discomfort that goes with being a Negro in a white neighborhood. Then came phone calls, cold, unfriendly.

The man from the corner stomped over and warned Mrs. Roberts that his kids had always played on their sidewalk and that nothing had better happen to them. She promised him that her children, ages 4, 5 (twins), 7 and 9, would not be violent to anyone.

Another man quit his bowling league, saying he was afraid to leave his wife at home with a Negro family in the neighborhood.

And there were the mean remarks to her children by other children in school and the glares of the neighbors when she went out.

Mrs. Roberts says she has tried to be a good neighbor. Or at least an inoffensive one.

Deliverymen were confused by The Sign and delivered the Bowdens' Christmas packages to her. Mrs. Roberts told them the sign was for people bearing rocks or bombs, not gifts.

She stopped shopping at the local supermarket and went to a distant Negro store because her presence offended the other customers. "They stared at me like I was some sort of freak."

She does not let her children out to play, so as not to terrify the neighbor who cherishes his sidewalk rights. They come straight home from school and stay inside or use the back yard. Maybe this summer they'll go out in front, she says, but she is not looking forward to it.

The Roberts even got rid of their dog because when it was in the yard it barked, which offended the neighbors. The kids cried, but their mutt went.

Mrs. Roberts says she does not want to be treated like a close relative. When she collapsed from nervousness and was hospitalized for a few days, she didn't expect any get-well cards and didn't get any.

But she would like her kids to be able to use their sidewalk and people to stop staring at her and her house.

"I'd really like to leave, but Charlie says he thinks we'll stay, so that means we'll stay. It doesn't bother him as much because he works two jobs and isn't here that much."

Then she laughed:

"Maybe I'll take the advice of a friend of mine. She said I should put up a sign just like the one next door except with the arrow pointing at them."

A Hero's Welcome

Some anti-busing ladies from the Northwest Side came downtown to picket us, which is OK. I believe in peaceful demonstration.

Some of the ladies had signs that asked why we aren't telling the truth. I thought we were, or were at least doing our best. They apparently think otherwise.

But if it is truth they want, here's a true story for them to think about.

Phillip Craig Skinner was young and black. But if white people can be believed, he was the kind of Negro, that rare kind, they wouldn't mind having live next door.

He never got in trouble. He went through Parker High School, studied, played football, was on the swimming team and graduated with good grades.

His generation is the generation of change, black power, black pride, militancy. But Phillip didn't get deeply involved in any organized movements.

When he finished high school, he enrolled in a Negro college in Missouri. He was getting good grades, but he left to join the United States Marine Corps.

Phillip went to Vietnam and was promoted to lance corporal. He wrote home often, to his father, a Chicago policeman and World War II vet, and his mother, who is divorced and remarried.

In his letters to his father, he wrote about his ambition to finish his military service and join his father as a policeman.

"When I get back from Vietnam, I'll go through police training," he wrote, "then we can be partners, Dad."

He didn't make it. While carrying a rocket launcher up a hill during fierce combat, he was shot in the head. He wasn't yet old enough to vote.

But he came close to becoming that clean, well-educated, law-abiding, public-spirited, polite, responsible, cultured, refined, lawn-tending Negro the white ladies say they

66

wouldn't mind having live next door to them—because they really don't believe he exists.

There is a little more to the story of Phillip. Being dead didn't change his skin color.

His mother tells it:

"After the Marine major left our living room, I asked my husband to call a funeral chapel to arrange for my son's burial.

"The man on duty said we could come to the chapel on appointment and furthermore that he was not sure the government provided good caskets for Vietnam victims. He felt certain that we would want to 'look over' his line.

"I called the chapel the next day to arrange for an appointment. Suddenly the impact of our ghetto address seemed to have struck home.

"There was some discussion over the phone as to why I had chosen that chapel, things to the effect that they had left this area when it had changed. Actually, they aren't very far from where we live and it is a nice funeral home.

"My husband visited the chapel. He was not led into the business office but was asked to wait in a dark corner of one of the parlors.

"The man scribbled some figures on a scratch pad and handed them to my husband, all the while explaining that 'While we are willing to handle this body, you understand, there are many excellent Negro undertakers on the South Side.' He went on about the chapels that 'would be near and convenient for the persons attending the wake.'

"By that time we were getting that feeling that Negroes acquire through a lifetime of such experiences—that of carrying a chip on their shoulder.

"So we did not inconvenience the white chapel by asking them to handle the body of a young man who gave the most there is to give.

"But I'll never understand what he gave it for. For that undertaker? Did he and other black boys give their lives in the hope that a few dozen black children could walk into a school without being spectacles? What did he give his life for?"

If anyone has a good answer to the question, I'll be glad to pass it on to Phillip's mother.

No Comment

Many people feel that busing is as much a moral issue as it is an educational device and a political football.

But you can't tell it from the Sunday sermons on the Northwest Side. Most clergymen there wouldn't touch it with a ten-foot candle.

A survey of some forty-five churches on the Northwest Side shows that only six clergymen have preached on busing since Superintendent James Redmond's plans got the area in an uproar.

About ten others say they have had informal talks with their congregations or have distributed "fact sheets."

But most have said nothing. And most of them say they will probably continue to say nothing.

One of the reasons for this silence is that many don't believe busing is a fit subject for a sermon. Others say that as policy they don't talk about current issues. A few indicate that busing is just too hot for them.

They don't even agree that it is a moral issue.

One Lutheran minister said: "I have not discussed it, nor do I think I will. Some of these things are not within the proper perspective of the church."

But another Lutheran minister, who plans a sermon on busing, said: ". . . as Christian citizens do we not have a responsibility to raise a moral voice within the community?"

Judging from what his fellow churchmen say, the answer to his question could be: "Yes," "No," "Maybe," "I don't know."

There's the viewpoint of the Rev. Roy E. Crawford, Austin Wesleyan Methodist Church, 500 N. Laramie. He thinks it is too "powerful" an issue for a church.

(I was under the impression that most churches are built on powerful issues.)

"I haven't discussed the subject in a sermon and I will not," he said. "I do not believe this belongs in the pulpit. Although it is true that we are a community church minister-

69

ing to the needs of the community, it is too powerful for the pulpit.

"We are right in the midst and this is something that could tear the congregation to pieces. We have people pulling both ways . . ."

A somewhat different opinion came from the Rev. Paul Buettner, of the Advent Lutheran Church, 1345 N. Karlov: "I haven't discussed it, but I feel that our negligence in not bringing this to the attention of the congregation does not speak well of any church."

Two Baptists provide an example of how not to see eye-to-eye.

The Rev. William E. Hakes, Galilee Baptist Church, 2958 N. Damen: "I don't think churches have a responsibility to discuss such issues."

The Rev. Clarence Walth, Foster Avenue Baptist Church, 5152 N. Mead: "I feel the church . . . has a moral responsibility."

A priest who preached a sermon on busing says he doesn't think it got anyone very high on brotherhood.

"The people here are mostly opposed to it," said the Rev. Paul Wisniewski, St. Cornelius Church, 5205 N. Lieb. "All I can do is try and keep trying to erase this blind spot—but it isn't easy."

And another priest, when busing was mentioned, said: "I don't have ANYTHING to say on THAT subject."

Is it a moral issue? Should it be discussed in a church? Two Lutherans give the answer:

The Rev. John P. Gaardsmoe, First Lutheran Church, 3500 W. Fullerton:

"My personal conviction is that in a church where you have many people gathered, it is not fair for me as a pastor to inflict my viewpoints on the congregation.

"If it is something from the gospel, that's different. That's my business. In social issues, I generally stick to the gospel."

The Rev. Leroy J. Iseminger, Lutheran Church of the Redeemer, 4901 N. Berenice:

"I've spoken to the congregation about it. My stand has been that we should approach the problem sanely and with a Christian attitude.

"If there is classroom space available, then certainly we should share it with those who need it. After all, we are our brothers' brothers and there is a moral issue here. As Christians, we should definitely be involved."

Since I don't partake regularly of their wisdom, I am in no position to comment on the judgment of clergymen or how they stimulate the conscience of their flocks.

But one thing about the racists and all-around haters, the fence-hopping congressmen and the nondescript aldermen: They know their issues when they see them, and they jump right in, muddy-feet first.

And once they are involved, it can't help but be a moral issue.

Some of My Best Customers . . .

One of the loudest anti-busing leaders on the Northwest Side is Steve Telow, head of the Kilbourn Association. Telow doesn't mince words. He is against his kids going to school with Negroes and he doesn't want Negroes living near him.

"My first loyalty is to the white Christian race," Telow says. "Anyone who would sell his house to a Negro or who favors busing is betraying white Christianity."

But don't get Telow wrong. He's not against Negroes in every way. He is not against their money. He makes a pretty good living from Negroes.

Telow likes to describe himself as a restaurant owner. Or as a food store operator.

But his business is the Smokey Hollow Tavern, 4333 W. Addison, a drab dump with a concrete floor and a bathroom that is out of service. He also sells sandwiches, hard-boiled eggs, milk, bread and packaged liquor.

In its own way, it is probably the strangest tavern in Chicago. It is in Telow's white neighborhood, where many of the residents support his Kilbourn organization.

It is a hangout for many of Telow's supporters, some of whom are outspoken racists. Somebody aptly called it "The Fritzel's of Bigotville."

But more than half of Telow's customers are Negroes. They work in nearby factories and launderies. It's the only tavern around, and Telow is willing to cash paychecks. So they stop there and spend money.

Wednesday was a typical day at Telow's bar. It was early in the afternoon, so the only customers were white. The Negroes don't drift in until they get off work, about four o'clock.

Harry the Politician came in about two o'clock and Telow poured him a beer. Harry is a Republican precinct captain and he used to be the chief elevator operator in the County Building. Now he has a job as a road repairman at the

County Highway Department, courtesy of Richard Ogilvie.

The county roads must have been in good shape because Harry was wearing casual clothes and he had two hours more to work. His work sheet for the day showed him working from 7 A.M. to 4 P.M. But from 2 to 4 P.M. he was at Telow's.

Harry is one of Telow's closest advisers and is at most of the anti-busing meetings and demonstrations. He was also very big against open housing.

One of the other customers slapped Harry on the back and respectfully said: "Harry, I seen you on TV again last week."

Harry shrugged. "Twenty-one times I been on TV."

"You're a real good politician, Harry. If you keep at it, you'll go places."

A bartender relieved Telow in mid-afternoon and he had time for a private chat about his views on life and the Negro.

First, the matter of his strong loyalty to "white Christianity." How strong is it? He was asked a hypothetical question: "What if you were a white Christian in Germany in the thirties and forties? Would you go along with the mass murder of the Jews?"

Telow thought about it. Finally: "Well, that's a tough question—but I think I would. That was their business, see, and they were just trying to preserve their culture. Yeah, I would have minded my own business about it."

Telow's white-Christian loyalty does not extend to such white Christians as Archbishop Cody, who favors busing.

"That goddam Cody," he said. "Go on, let's see if you got the guts to print that!"

He considers Cody to be as dangerous to society as Mayor Daley or Martin Luther King. He even uses them to advertise his food. His walls are covered with such racist witticisms as:

"King-Daley-Cody Troika Eggs, 2 for 15 cents." And: "Kosher chitterlins by Rabbi King—good and tastey." And this gem: "Human relations miscegated homogenized mixed-blood sausage sandwich."

The signs don't bother his Negro customers, Telow said. "See, most of them agree with me. I mean it. They do.

"You got to understand, I'm not really against them. I just don't think the two cultures should mix. And I also think they are reproducing too fast. They are going to overrun us at the rate they are going."

Telow's voice rises when he talks about Negroes' having babies. This, more than anything, offends Telow—the father of four children.

"I'd like to see a law that there be electric lights in all public housing apartments that stay on twenty-four hours a day. And that they got to have TV sets in the bedrooms. You see, Negroes don't like to make love with the lights on. They prefer darkness. So that would cut down the birth rate." He did not appear to be joking.

Taxes also irritate Telow. He feels Negroes don't pull their share of the load. "I pay mine. I pay $750 a year on my home. But do they pay theirs?"

Since he brought up the subject of taxes, I asked him why the state had to yank him into court to make him pay about $1,400 in sales tax he collected from customers but didn't pass on.

"You know about that, huh?" said Telow. "Sure—I'm a conniver. I admit it. You got to connive and cheat to make ends meet. I learned it from watching the guys downtown."

Telow tried to make it in politics, but things haven't worked out. "I was a Democratic precinct captain, but they didn't like my views and kicked me out of the organization. I was a Republican precinct captain and carried my precinct for Waner. But they don't like my views and kicked me out. They're both alike. They don't let a guy have his own opinions."

It was four o'clock, quitting time at the factories and laundries and several black men came in.

"How you all," drawled Harry the Politician, the hard-working highway repairman.

Big Eddy, a tall, husky Negro smiled sweetly and said: "And how are things here in KKK headquarters with all you lily-white racists." Everybody laughed and Telow gave a look that seemed to say "See? We all get along; we joke."

Later, Big Eddy and a few others talked about Telow and why they spend their money in his place. "Main reason is it's the only place around here. It's a place to get a cool one after work and he'll cash a paycheck if you spend a little.

"We know how he feels and he knows how we feel. We even had a picket line outside his place once. But, what the hell, he wouldn't be as bad as he is if he didn't listen to Harry. That's where he gets a lot of those racist ideas.

"But you know something? We are hurtin' that man. How? With love. We don't let his talk bother us and we love him in return and that hurts him. That's L-O-V-E, brother. You can win a lot more with love than you can with hate. And they can't understand that. That's why they are hurtin'."

Telow tossed their money into his cash register. One of them dropped a quarter in the jukebox. Someone else ordered a couple of sandwiches.

If the love and tolerance of his Negro customers were causing him pain, Telow was taking it like a Spartan.

A Flip of the Ethnic Coin

I ran into Mr. Brown, a Negro business executive, and was sorry to find that he is no longer a moderate in racial matters. He has become an extremist and nothing I said could alter his thinking.

"Do you know the answer to the problems of busing and open housing and other such issues?" he asked.

I told him that I wished I did.

"The answer is to put all those people on boats and send them back to Europe, that's what."

You must be joking, I suggested.

"No. These people have no respect for our laws and the American way of life. Maybe if they went to Russia or Poland or Lithuania or Latvia or one of those other Communist countries, they'd be happier. So we should send them back to where they come from."

I argued that these people are just as American as Mr. Brown.

"Oh, yeah? Then why don't they have any respect for the U.S. Supreme Court? Why don't they have any respect for the laws created by the legislative branch, approved by the executive branch and upheld by the judicial branch of our government?"

You must understand, I told Mr. Brown, that many of these people aren't fortunate enough to be as well educated as you—to have gone through college where they could learn about our system of government.

Mr. Brown shouted: "That's because they are lazy. I pulled myself up by my bootstraps and went through college. I read books. You can get books in the library. But these people don't want to educate themselves or work hard enough to go to night school and learn something.

"And do you know why? Because all they want to do is go out on Friday nights when they get paid and dance the polka, or whatever their native dance is, drink shots and beers and get in fights.

76

"And the ones who don't do that—all they want to do is sit home in front of TV and watch cowboys, drink beer and wait for their union to get them a raise."

That's a terrible stereotype, I told Mr. Brown. They aren't all like that.

"Ninety per cent of them are. I know those people. I've worked with them. I was in the service with them. Sometimes I sit next to them on the CTA, if there is no way I can avoid it. And you know what? They have a funny smell."

What?

"It's true. They all smell of garlic. They put garlic in everything they eat. I don't know how they can stand being around each other. Ugh.

"And another thing. Why can't they learn how to speak like Americans if they are going to live in this country? I hear them saying 'dis' and 'dat,' 'dem' and 'dose.' Or they call their mother their 'mither.'

"Some of 'em even talk in foreign languages—jibberish, I call it. If they are going to be Americans, they ought to learn to talk like Americans, not like a bunch of Commies."

Just a moment. That's unfair, to start accusing people of being Communists . . .

"Oh, it is, is it? You bleeding-heart liberals are all alike. Has it ever occurred to you that all of the countries they have come from have gone either Communist or Socialist?

"Look at Poland and those other Slavic tribes. And half of Germany. They all went Commie. Italy has got Commies all over the place. They even hold public offices. And most of the rest of Europe is Socialist in one way or another."

That doesn't mean Americans from those countries are like that.

"Listen, it is in their blood. Those people just aren't ready for Democracy. They just don't know how to live in a democratic society. Ship 'em back on the next boat, that's what I say."

Nonsense. I refuse to listen to such . . .

"And what about those gangsters—the Bossa Costra, the syndicate? They are nothing but savages, shooting each other and stuffing each other in sewers and trunks. Don't tell me they aren't savage hordes at heart."

But they are just a minority. Not at all typical. Besides, many of them came from poor neighborhoods and turned to anti-social behavior because their upward mobility was blocked by social and economic discrimination.

"More bleeding heart. Listen, pal, I came from a poor neighborhood, too. I don't stuff people in trunks and sewers. I'm not in the Cassa Nova. I mean it—violence is in their blood. Just tell me how many international wars my people have been in, compared to those violent groups."

You are a bigot.

"See? Every time someone gives you the straight facts based on his experiences, you call him a bigot. But you have to admit one thing."

What?

"Those people don't have any rhythm."

Ladies' Day

It was a beautiful morning, crisp and clear. On such a morning the neighborhood around the Sayre School takes on added beauty because the homes are a deep, rich brown and trees form archways over the quiet streets.

Sayre is a traditional-looking school. Big, made of dark yellow bricks, surrounded by shrubbery. It fills half the block. The rest is open, fenceless school yard. The effect is that of a village square.

Nobody was on the street. Most men had left earlier. Inside the houses, the women were getting the kids ready for school.

At 8:10 the school janitor came out and hauled the flag up the pole. Teachers, most of them looking motherly, arrived in cars.

Two patrolboys sauntered toward their corners, slipping on yellow chest-belts. They talked about what everyone in the neighborhood was talking about—the Negro kids who would be coming that morning.

The shorter boy said: "My mom says she doesn't care if they come here to school but she doesn't want me to go anywhere on a bus. I guess that's how I feel. I don't care who comes to school here. It doesn't bother me."

His friend, already a six-footer, nodded. "There won't be any trouble, I don't think. We don't have any really tough kids at Sayre—just me and one other."

It was 8:40 and kids were gathering in the playground; more than you'd expect to find that early.

When they talked about the busing, they followed a pattern.

First they said the things they heard at home. Then they thought for themselves and sounded more intelligent.

One round-faced blond boy ("I'm Polish. We're mostly Italian or Polish here.") looked serious as he said:

"I don't mind going to school with them. But I don't like all those taxes being spent for them to ride buses."

His buddy hooted and laughed. "What taxes do you pay? Ha, you talking about paying taxes."

The round-faced boy tried to sustain his serious composure. But he, too, laughed.

That's the way the talk went. First the lesson of the kitchen table: "Taxes. . . . Why don't they improve their own schools? . . . OUR neighborhood. . . . They'll slow us down. . . . They'd better not try anything rough. . . ."

Then thoughts of their own: "Maybe they'll be OK and we can be friends. . . . I don't care and it might be fun. . . . I'll treat them nice and they'll treat us nice. . . ."

At 8:50 the school buzzer gave its first ring. Traffic thickened as mothers dropped kids off. Many parked and waited.

Then came the sign wavers, about a dozen women in their mid- and late thirties. The signs were intended to let the Negro children know they weren't wanted—at least by this group of ladies.

They were led by a bleached blond who insists, whenever we meet, that she is not a bigot.

After displaying the signs for the cameras, she said knowingly: "I suppose you know they burned the medical records of these colored kids?"

Why would they do that?

"Disease. And not the kind you get by being breathed on, either." Her friends nodded.

What kind of disease?

"Do you have daughters? Well, if you did, you'd know what I'm talking about and you'd be worried, too."

Are you talking about venereal disease?

"That's right," she said triumphantly. "Veeeee-Deeeeee." And her friends nodded again.

There they stood on a beautiful morning, while the flag flapped above them, convincing each other that some sixth-grade school children were bringing VD into their neighborhood.

At 9 o'clock the school buzzer rang again. The bus hadn't arrived yet.

"See," a fat woman said. "They're late. Now they are going to come in and disturb MY kids."

Then it was suddenly there, rolling up the street. The ladies got their signs up. Others, without signs, spread out along the sidewalk.

But the bus went by, turned a corner and made for the back door. For a moment the ladies didn't realize what was happening. "Are they going around the block?"

Then they realized and they ran. Whatever feminine qualities they had simply vanished as they trotted and jiggled with their signs held aloft, angry that the Negro children might get inside without seeing their message.

The bus stopped and the first child, about 10, came out. He looked around and blinked. Then he forced a smile. His teeth chattered. It might have been the cold. Or it might not.

The ladies stood 50 feet away, blocked by a tall police sergeant. They stared open-mouthed for a few seconds. Then, as an attendant lined the kids up, a woman said in a doomsday voice: "Well, they're here. They're here."

They marched into the school and the heavy door closed behind them. They were there, all right.

Some of the mothers left. But others waited in angry clusters. One saw a reporter who had talked to some children. "Are you proud of yourself," she hissed "interviewing children?" She made it sound like he had committed a deviate act.

At 10:30 recess began. They poured out and played jump rope, basketball, kick-ball, or just ran. You had to look close to see the Negro kids. They weren't clustered. A little girl waited for her turn to jump rope. A dark little boy was chased by a white boy. The white boy tagged him and the dark boy gave chase. Both laughed.

The grim ladies on the sidewalk talked about Communists, Redmond, the press, Hugh Hill, crime rates, secession and other weighty matters.

A group of boys played a game kicking a basketball. One kid kicks. The others try to catch it on the fly. The one who catches it gets the next kick.

One Negro boy played. After ten kicks he hadn't made a catch. He was hanging back shyly, not plunging into the crowd for the ball. But he seemed happy.

Finally, near the end of recess, the ball came his way. But a tall white boy was closer. The white boy started for it, glanced back, then jumped aside. The black boy caught it and got his kick.

When recess ended, they were walking back together, talking easily. They had run and whooped and yelled together, as children should.

And through it all, the grim ladies stood on the sidewalk and bemoaned the great tragedy that had been visited upon them.

But they had only each other to tell it to. Their kids were inside, finding out that things aren't always the way they hear it around the kitchen table.

LIVE AND LET LIVE

The Hobo and the Hippie

There is a lot of interest in the hippie movement so I thought I would go out and interview one.

Luck was with me. I spotted a man on a bridge near the Loop who was a perfect specimen of the hippie.

He was wearing a stubble of beard, long sideburns, old tennis shoes, overalls and an Ike jacket.

Excuse me, I said, but how long ago did you drop out of society?

"Oh, a very long time ago."

You choose to wear unusual clothing. Why?

"These are the only clothes I have."

Do you like to get high?

"Yes, sir. I try to get high every day."

And you believe in peace?

"Yep. I don't bother nobody and I don't like nobody to bother me."

Your living conditions—are they drab, barren, simple?

"Just a dumpy, dirty old room is all."

Well, you are a real genuine hippie, aren't you?

"Hippie? No. I'm an old-fashioned Skid Row bum. I'm just standing here on this bridge trying to mooch quarters for wine."

A bum? But you fit the description of a hippie perfectly. You have dropped out, you dress in strange clothing, you get high, you are peace-loving.

"Yes, people are always making that mistake because the two groups are so similar. But there are some very basic differences."

Such as?

"We are a much, much older culture. There have been drunken bums dropping out, getting high, minding their own business for centuries. So it is very unfair."

What is unfair?

"All the publicity and attention they are getting. I go in a bar and look at the TV set and there is a useless, lazy bum, half-high on marijuana, being interviewed about Vietnam, the President and other things.

"I'm just as useless and lazy as any hippie, and I get just as high on wine as he does on marijuana. But am I invited on television talk shows to give my opinions? No. The only time anybody asks me anything is when the judge asks if I want to go to the jail or to the work farm for my thirty days.

"And look how dedicated we are. The average hippie is going to stick with it for a few months, a year or two maybe, then he will shave, get a job, get married, buy a house in the suburbs and tell me to beat it when I ask him for a quarter near the commuter station. But most of us old-fashioned bums are in it for life.

"Do people treat us nicely the way they treat hippies? Of course not. If a hippie goes in a park and plays loud rock 'n' roll music and throws flowers at people and dances, it is called a 'Be-In' or a 'Love-In.'

"But if I go in a park and just sit on a bench it is called loitering.

"If I go up to the University of Chicago and stand around, the intellectuals will say: 'There is a bum. Arrest him.' But if they see a hippie standing around the same way, they will say: 'Oh, you are the hope of the world. Please throw a daisy at me.'"

Why don't you become a hippie?

"I have my pride. And I prefer wine to marijuana or LSD. It tastes better.

"Besides, I don't have a college education and I don't come from a comfortable family background, so I can't qualify socially as a hippie.

"Why, if I went around to where the hippies live they'd just say, 'Scat, you bum.'

"But I've often thought about what it would be like today if my parents had had the money in the old days to put me through college and give me a proper upbringing.

"I sure wouldn't be no dirty, unshaven bum, standing

on this bridge mooching quarters for wine so I can get high.

"No sir. I'd be a dirty, unshaven hippie, cashing my allowance check from my dad so I can buy some pot and get high.

"Just shows what a difference the advantages can make."

Love Me, Love My Rock

A hippie with a guitar case slung over his shoulder and a hippie girl at his side walked up to a bus counter at O'Hare Airport a few days ago and asked for two tickets to the Loop.

Miss Maureen Ryan, the ticket girl, gave him the tickets and asked for four dollars.

The young man reached into a jacket pocket and took out a rock and two seashells. He pushed them toward Miss Ryan.

"What is this?" Miss Ryan asked.

"A rock," he said, "and two seashells."

"I can see that."

"I don't believe in paper money," the young man said. "All the trouble in the world is caused by paper money."

Miss Ryan pointed out that her company was not troubled by paper money. It likes it. But, she said, it didn't believe in rocks. So she wanted four dollars.

The hippie said: "If a person really wants something, it should be paid for with an object he loves, not with some meaningless paper.

"I have treasured this rock for many years. I love this rock."

"What about the seashells?" Miss Ryan asked.

"I love them, too."

Miss Ryan said she was touched. She had not met many people who loved a plain, gray rock. But she pointed out that her boss might not believe that the rock was worth four dollars in unloved money. "I mean, how can anyone really tell about a rock?"

"I see what you are driving at," the hippie said. "Yes, I understand your problem. All right, if you don't think it is worth four dollars, the answer is really simple: You give me some change."

He was a very sly hippie.

Miss Ryan, joining in the spirit of the moment, walked

around her desk and went outside for a while. She came back and put some pebbles in front of the hippie.

"There's your change."

The hippie shook his head. "No, no, you don't love those pebbles. They mean nothing to you. How can you insult me by giving me unloved pebbles in exchange for my best rock?"

"But these are my favorite pebbles," Miss Ryan insisted. "I bring them to work with me so I can be near them."

"I don't believe you," the hippie said. "You're just saying that."

A line had formed, including several non-hippies who stared with open mouths as they listened to the discussion. Miss Ryan finally told the hippie that she would have to have four dollars, even if it was in unloved, detested money, if he wanted the tickets.

"Give me my rock back," the hippie snapped. As he turned to leave, he pointed at Miss Ryan's uniform and said:

"You should not wear a uniform, you know. Uniforms do not promote love."

An elderly man standing in line glared at the hippie and snapped:

"Uniform? What do you think of straightjackets, that's what I'd like to know."

The hippie gave a loving wave, and he and his girlfriend got in a cab and left.

It is presumed they did not offer the most-loved rock to the cab driver in lieu of his fare, as there have been no reports from hospitals about a hippie with a cracked head.

A New Breed of Bum

A hippie named Dave dropped in the other day. As there were no flies coming out of his beard, I invited him to sit and ferment awhile.

After a bit of small talk about how much better the world will be after everybody over thirty dies off, we got down to the reason for his visit.

It seems some of Dave's hippie friends have heard about something called work. They want to try it, even though they know it isn't something they can smoke.

I'm always willing to help someone find work, so I reached for the want ad section.

Dave said it wouldn't be of use to his hippie friends. The kind of jobs they want aren't found in the want ads.

Besides, employers are always asking them to get haircuts and to wear something less fashionable than beads and a Civil War cap.

"Our people want jobs where they can creatively be themselves," Dave said. "They want work that will let them express themselves. They don't want a straight gig."

What's a straight gig?

"They wouldn't fit into something like an insurance company. They'd be qualified, of course, because many are well educated, with BA's. One even has a PhD.

"But they don't want something like that. They are primarily creative people who have difficulty getting jobs because of their appearance, political views or something that makes them unacceptable by establishment standards."

I pointed out that the establishment doesn't care much how somebody looks while working a car wash, digging a ditch, picking grapefruit and other such jobs, many of which are available.

"These are creative people," Dave repeated.

Because society is stifling the creativity of Dave's friends, and because of their disdain for straight gigs, they have formed the Hip Job Co-op.

This means they sit around a storefront in Old Town, waiting for someone to offer them a creative, self-fulfilling job.

And in order to let the world know that this great pool of creativity is waiting to be tapped, Dave seeks publicity for the venture.

The idea is that if I write about it, you, the reader, will rush to the phone to hire one of these creative creatures.

This is something like the setup on Skid Row, where there are offices that will rent out drifters by the day for manual labor.

The difference is, the drifter on Skid Row has no choice because he is short on education and brains and long on thirst.

Dave's creative drifters are a different breed of bum. He's an example.

Dave is twenty-two. He was raised in Lake Forest, the richest of our suburbs. His father is a wealthy corporate executive.

After knocking around a few colleges and deciding that life in Lake Forest is no good, Dave dropped out of things to become a hippie.

(Poor youths also get fed up with their way of life and drop out of things. But they usually do so by enlisting.)

Since Dave asked me to help, I'll do what I can. And what I can do is suggest that we all get together and ignore Dave and his friends.

If somebody is looking for help, I urge hiring a man in his forties or fifties who has been squeezed out of a job by automation, a shake-up, a merger or for some other reason. Men in these age brackets are having a hard time finding jobs. I'm sure many of them are creative and, since most are balding, getting a haircut won't be an issue.

Or, hire a kid from the ghettos. There's as much creativity there as along the North Shore. You have to be creative just to avoid jail or the grave.

I am not enthusiastic about Dave and his friends for a couple of reasons.

For one thing, I doubt if they are as creative as they think they are.

They like to preach about love, smoke odd things, take acid trips, wear flowers, use obscenities and whoop it up sexually. This, they conclude, makes them sensitive, creative souls.

Most genuinely creative people are too busy creating to have much time left for goofing around or talking about how creative they are.

The other problem with Dave and his pals is mom's station wagon. They are still waiting for it.

It was always there when they were growing up. It took them to the parties, to school, to the private lessons, everywhere. And dad was there to pick up the tab.

When they became hippies they proved only that they didn't need mom's station wagon to go out in the world and do absolutely nothing.

But now that they want to do something, like work, they are waiting for the station wagon again.

Sorry, kid, I'm not your mom. Start walking.

Shock Proof

The most important thing in the life of a hippie is not his pot or even another hippie. It is the person who gets angry, shocked or nervous when a hippie appears.

That's when a hippie is really happy—when someone looks with gaping jaw or gritting teeth. Getting reactions from non-hippies makes hippies as happy as babies playing peek-a-boo.

And the sight of a silly kid who has run away from the suburbs in order to wear funny clothes and/or long hair unnerves some people, although not as many as it once did.

This is what hippies seem to always talk about, at least in the presence of non-hippie newsmen.

They tell their stories just the way youthful drinkers proudly boast and giggle about how drunk they were, how sick they got, how foolish they acted and how hungover they are.

Tuesday was a day for hippie storytelling. Some hippie leaders from New York came to town and joined local hippies in requesting a city permit to use Grant Park during the Democratic convention in August.

Asking for a permit is an easy enough thing to do. One person can do it. But the hippies turned it into a major non-event event. Their lives are full of such non-events.

In the morning they gathered at the Old Town office of the *Seed*, the local hippie paper.

While one or two of them drafted the park-use request, the others jabbered about the different ways they have shocked people.

One told how he and a hippie friend went on a guided tour of the New York Stock Exchange. Once inside, they tossed money about. This, I gathered, has symbolic value. The money-tossing shocked people. And the memory of it brought gales of laughter from the hippie storyteller and his audience.

93

On the way to the park district headquarters, a hippie leader told how he shocked people at San Francisco's airport.

A woman was brought to the airport dressed in a nun's habit. When the hippie leader got to the airport to go somewhere, the woman kissed him good-by with great passion.

This, he disclosed, shocked the observers, and has great significance. He didn't explain what the significance was, but I gather that it indicated most people are surprised when they see someone in a nun's habit smooching with a hippie at an airport: a profound discovery, indeed.

As they trotted around Chicago Tuesday, the small group giggled at the attention they received. Actually, they didn't get much, but they thought they did.

The mayor wasn't able to see them but they enjoyed teasing one of his aides. The aide was rather poised. Anyone who hangs around aldermen can't be surprised by a few hippies.

The thing they are planning for this summer is aimed at shocking Chicago's non-hips, which most of us are. The hippies are already giggling about how they will make everyone's eyes bug out at the sight of tens of thousands of them camping in Grant Park for a week.

There they will play games, frolic, make music or love, toss flowers at each other, turn on, turn off—but most important, they will shock us.

The mayor should not hesitate to give them a park permit. They'll come anyway if he doesn't, so he may as well make it legal and avoid the formality of tossing a few of them in jail.

The hippies, I suspect, will find Chicago is not quite the same as San Francisco, last summer's headquarters. It's not as easily captivated by fads, excited by goofs or shocked.

Shocked? A city that has had Capone and Accardo, dead bodies and dead alewives, Calumet City and Marina City, Lar Daly and Mayor Daley, beer riots and race riots isn't going to be fazed by a horde of kids with long hair and beads.

The hippies might even serve a useful purpose. The city's jackrollers and assorted creeps will converge on Grant Park, thus making the streets much safer.

The teen-age gangs will probably declare a truce in their personal war and go over to the park to tap a few flower children on their tousled tops.

Let them have the park, Mr. Mayor. At the end of the week all that will remain of the sweet young things is a tuft of hair and a bead or two.

The Hippies Are Coming,
The Hippies Are Coming

Hippies want us to think that we are goofy and they are normal. That is just hippie propaganda. They are trying to shake our normal values.

A good example of how goofy hippies are and how normal we are can be found in the 7600 block of North Paulina.

Until recently, this was a normal street, with normal businesses in the stores and normal people in the flats upstairs.

Then Marvin rented one of the stores. He is a hippie. He is the first hippie ever to go into business in the block. He is the first hippie many of the people there ever saw.

Marvin opened a hippie store. He sells hippie things, such as slogan-buttons; pop art posters; tinted, distorted glasses; hippie bumper stickers and hippie underground newspapers.

Marvin is twenty-seven, funny-looking with his long sideburns, big mustache and tiny glasses, and is an Army veteran.

During the day he works delivering groceries, and two teen-age hippies run the store until he gets there. They are Marc, 17, and Marcia, 18, who say they are in love and will marry when Marc earns enough so he doesn't need the $25-a-week allowance from his lawyer-father.

Many businessmen on the block and residents of the nearby apartment buildings are terribly upset by Marvin's store. The owner of Marvin's building is trying to evict him. People constantly call the police and make anonymous complaints. The police are always pulling up and looking at Marvin's store.

Marvin is accused of the following offenses: Being un-American (his discharge papers are in the window), selling obscene material (some of his buttons are crude; most are satirically funny), playing his stereo set too loud (he admits having done this but says he will keep it turned down), running a hangout for hippies (hippies have come to the store; so have normal people), preaching love and peace (he admits it), and looking goofy (he admits that, too).

As you can see, it is no surprise that the normal people in the neighborhood are all upset by Marvin's store.

It was a fine normal block until Marvin came in. It has seven taverns and the customers are perfectly normal, sometimes getting falling-down drunk, having fist fights, swearing, making loud noises until 2 A.M., wrecking their livers, blowing their paychecks, playing the jukebox too loud.

Because they are normal, not goofy like Marvin and his friends, they don't like him.

One of the tavern customers even told Marvin off good a few days ago. The man and his wife staggered out of the tavern and stood outside Marvin's store. He made a beautiful speech:

"You are un-American," he cried.

"I served in the Army," Marvin said.

"Yeah, but you didn't fight. You didn't lose a leg."

"I'm glad I didn't lose a leg," Marvin said.

"See?" the man shouted. "I told you you are un-American."

Then there is the matter of Marvin's posters and buttons. Most of them carry slogans like:

"Chicken Little Was Right."

"Cancer Stops Smoking."

But some of them have four-letter words, which offend the people in the area, who have never seen or heard such words before.

Until Marvin came along, nobody sold posters or buttons with four-letter words on them.

The only place you could read four-letter words was in

the books you can buy in the paperback rack in the neighborhood drugstore. It has some of the bluest novels on the market.

But that is where normal people expect to find dirty words and smut—in a drugstore paperback rack, not in a hippie store.

Marvin says he is going to battle his landlord in court if the eviction threat is carried out.

He doesn't realize, apparently, that if he stays there too long, he might become as normal as his neighbors are.

And that proves just how goofy Marvin really is.

The "Seed" Transplanted

The most interesting relationship in publishing history is not to be.

The Chicago Tribune Company has decided it doesn't want one of its suburban subsidiaries to print the *Seed*.

The *Seed* is the voice of Chicago's hippie, just as the *Tribune* is the voice of his grandfather.

In recent months, the *Seed* has been printed by Merrill Printing Company, Hinsdale. But on January 18, the *Tribune* announced it had bought Merrill. And last week Merrill told the *Seed*'s editors they don't want their printing business anymore.

"They told us it was the policy of the new owners not to print the *Seed*," said Colin Pearlson, *Seed* editor. "I was surprised because I do not see that policy in the *Tribune*'s platform for a greater Chicago."

Pearlson said he is looking for another firm to print the *Seed*, which sells about 24,000 papers a week.

It is too bad the *Tribune* feels the way it does because the *Seed* is, after all, a newspaper and it tries to provide a service for its readers.

Like most papers, it prints news, editorials, columns, want ads, letters from its readers and most of the other things papers contain.

It just happens to look at life a little differently than does the *Tribune*. Much of its news is about smoking pot, who has been pinched and all that. And much of it sounds like it has been written by someone smoking pot. The *Tribune* writers, on the other hand, do not sound like they are stimulated by pot or much of anything.

Both papers seize upon many current subjects for their editorials. But they take slightly different positions.

Take the subject of rioting. The *Tribune*'s editorials usually suggest stern punishment for rioters. Maybe dropping them from zeppelins.

But when the *Seed* offices were stoned by Waller High rioters, it responded in this flower-child way:

"How can we editorialize against this action of our black brothers. Smashing windows is a reflex action of the (censored) they have to take every day. . . . Let he among you who is without sin pick up that brick and throw it back."

Many of the *Seed*'s pages are filled with long, rambling, petulant and sometimes incoherent outcries against all the things it finds wrong with the world. Quite unlike the *Tribune*.

But the *Seed* features sometimes have a sprightly quality. And it is assumed they interest the *Seed*'s readers, who don't seem interested in much besides pot.

There are do-it-yourself hints. The *Seed* recently explained how to convert a telephone into a pipe for smoking pot.

Its gardening advice usually deals with how best to grow your own marijuana.

There was even a cooking recipe in a recent edition.

"Cut lemon in half, put in pan, bake at 250 degrees F for about 10-15 minutes. Take out of oven, squeeze lemon into pan, replace in oven until completely dry, throw away dried skins, scrape up black substance in pan, grind up, mix with tobacco in a cigaret. It works. Watch out for limes."

The *Seed*, like the *Tribune*, has a restaurant columnist, who recently wrote: "Another shattering experience. The delicatessen on Grand Avenue just east of St. Clair.

"There's one counter man there who screams at everybody. All the others scream, too, but this particular one MEANS it, and he's so violent that people scream back.

"My own reaction was to retreat almost in tears. How is it possible for one man to radiate pure malevolence for nine feet in all directions, I don't know, but this cat does it.

"The horrible thing is that the customers like the screaming. They go there to be screamed at. As for me, I'm not going back, no matter how good the corned beef is."

There is one area in which the *Seed* surpasses the *Tribune* or any other paper. And that is in the quality of its classified ads. That may be why the *Tribune* dropped the *Seed:* jealousy.

Here are some samples:

"Student at large, will sell mind, body and/or soul to the devil or any other interested party."

"Will support chick, preferably under 25 with child or two."

"Kathy from Janey. Get in touch. You owe me $10."

"The most exotic, sophisticated and functional Hash Pipe ever handcrafted. Send $2 to the Zok shop."

"Get High, not burned. Save your lips and fingertips. Use a Zok-Joint. The perfect portable joint holder. Stylish, practical."

And a satisfied advertiser sent in this testimonial to *Seed*'s selling power:

"Since we placed our *Seed* unclassified, our phone hasn't stopped ringing. We've heard from every freak in town."

Basically, the philosophical difference between the *Seed* and the *Tribune* comes down to one unusual item.

As a spontaneous expression of youthful joy, the *Seed* recently said:

"Yippee! Yippee! Yippee! Yippee! Yippee! Yippee! Yippee! Yippee! Yippee! Yippee! Yippee! Yippee! Yippee! Yippee! Yippee! Yippee!"

That's all there was to the news item.

I doubt if the *Tribune* would ever do something like that. But it would be fun seeing "harrumph" sixteen times.

Letter from the Front

(Here is a letter from a fighting man, sent to his parents back home.)

"Dear Mom, Dad, Billy, Sis and Spot:

"I hope this letter will get to you, but I'm not sure it will.

"We are trapped. Completely surrounded, outnumbered.

"Right now, it's quiet. But we know they are up to something. They are out there somewhere, the dirty, no-good (censored).

"I'm writing this just before dawn. That's when we expect them to hit. If my handwriting is hard to read, it's because there's no light. They knocked that out.

"It's hot as hell here. I haven't washed in almost a week. We've been here for three days.

"None of us has eaten in almost twenty-four hours. Believe me, no matter what you've seen on television or read in the papers, this is even rougher.

"It's kind of a funny feeling knowing that I don't have to be here, that I could be back home, safe and comfortable.

"In your last letter you asked me: 'Son, why did you have to do it? Why did you have to join?'

"Mom—you didn't raise your son to be a coward.

"I'm here because there are thousands of other guys all over this country doing the same thing.

"And when Bruce came into the student lounge and said, 'Guys, we are going to take over the administration building and seize the dean's office,' I put down my guitar, put on my psychedelic beads and joined up.

"I couldn't sit by, knowing that at dozens of campuses, thousands of guys were fighting for their right to hire and fire the faculty, to determine what they will learn and to live off-campus with a girl, while here, there was nothing going on.

"Maybe you can understand how I felt when I'd look around this, my campus, and see people going to class, leaving that class and going to another one, then going back to their rooms to study.

"I've never seen such complacency.

"Worst of all, the man sitting in the dean's office was the dean.

"Mom, Dad—that's tyranny.

"If I sat back and let it continue, it would make my draft deferment meaningless.

"Now maybe you folks who are home-side understand what it's like here and why we're doing what we're doing. It's a dirty business, I know, but it has to be done.

"Oh, you read that we're the ones doing the dirty stuff— spilling the dean's ink, smoking his cigars.

"I know you've read that we shouldn't be in the dean's office in the first place—that we should get out of the dean's office now.

"Believe me, we've tried to negotiate. But they won't surrender.

"The people who say these things are probably sincere, but they are just dupes of the international conspiracy of deans.

"If we get out of the dean's office, then everything here will fall—the cafeteria, the squash courts, the ladies' room.

"That's why we must make our stand here and now or we will be overrun by the authoritarian hordes. We'll spend the rest of our lives in chains, taking orders from deans, bosses, wives, tax collectors and traffic cops—the whole bit.

"Well, I've got to close now. I can hear them. They're coming for us. Any minute now they will be all over us.

"But, by gosh, they aren't going to take me without a struggle. I'm a good 230 pounds, and some cop is going to get a hernia carrying me to the wagon."

Just Like the Old Country

The police were cracking the heads of war protesters in Oakland, California, the other day and squirting stuff in their eyes, and I say it is about time.

There's nothing that gets me as mad as some no-good, troublemaking, draft-dodging draft-dodger like Joan Baez and her mother.

Just the other day I heard somebody play one of her songs on the radio about peace and nonviolence and love, and I called that station and asked them why they were trying to cause trouble.

Here this country has got its hands full trying to preserve freedom in Vietnam. How can we do that if our own people won't shut up and do what they're told.

We've got to get this war over with so's our boys can come home. But we can't ever get this war over and bring our boys home if every time you turn around some goofy peacenik is saying that we've got to get this war over and bring our boys home.

Those people don't realize that if we don't fight communism in Vietnam, pretty soon we're going to have it right here. And if that ever happens, just let those people try to protest. They'll find out that you can't get away with that under communism. The Commies will split their heads and squirt stuff in their eyes.

The trouble with those punks is that they got it too easy. They don't know what it's like to have some hard knocks. They should talk to my old man or your old man, right?

Like my old man came over here from the Old Country because things were no good over there. He didn't have no freedom.

Now when he looks at his TV and sees those people complaining, he says they ought to put 'em all in jail and throw away the key. That's what they used to do to troublemakers in the Old Country. Like he says, that's the trouble with this country—people get away with too much.

You know what I think we ought to do with them? We ought to put them on a boat and send them all to Russia. Let them see how they like it over there, getting their heads cracked and stuff squirted in their eyes every time they open their mouths. Then they'd appreciate the freedom they got here and wouldn't open their mouths to complain.

It's not just the punks that get me mad, either. Sometimes I see guys like that Sen. Fulbright on TV and I could kick my picture tube in, except I wouldn't give him the satisfaction.

Now there's a United States senator standing up criticizing what the President is doing. When that happens, you got to wonder what this country is coming to.

Did you see that mother on TV—the one who has got a boy in the Army. She really told off some of the anti-war protesters. She told them how she is willing for him to go there and give up his life if he has to. That woman is willing for her boy to give up his life, which is a mother's privilege, so why can't the protesters shut up about not wanting him to. Did any of them ever give up their boy's life?

You bet they didn't, especially Joan Baez or Sen. Fulbright. All they do is go around complaining about somebody else's boy.

I say we got to get behind our boys, just like Howard Wally said on the radio this morning. These people ought to stop complaining and start waving flags and writing letters to the boys.

I sent a letter the other day and told some kid over there that I'm right here behind him waving my flag and not to let his spirit get low because as far as I'm concerned he should stay there until the job gets done and not to pay any attention to people who talk about ending the war and bringing him home.

Super-Doopers vs. Joan Baez

We have just finished observing Kick Joan Baez Week in Chicago.

This is always a big event for the super-dooper patriots. It happens whenever Miss Baez comes to Chicago or any other town.

Something about the slim, dark-haired singer raises their love of country to the fervor of a lynch mob.

They rage about everything from her hairdo to the shocking fact that she is paid well enough for her singing to afford the better hotels.

There are few people that the super-dooper patriots dislike more than Miss Baez. They even think she is as bad as Dr. Spock, which is very bad indeed.

But I have never understood why they feel this way. I have read about most of the things that Miss Baez believes in, and I don't think they are much different, basically, than the things the super-dooper patriots believe in.

In fact, Miss Baez and the SDP's agree on many key issues. They just don't realize it.

Take the issue of nonviolence, which Miss Baez is very interested in. She is nonviolent herself and encourages others to be the same.

You could kick Miss Baez right in her guitar and she probably wouldn't do a thing, she feels that strongly about it. She even runs a school for nonviolence in California. The fact that people can now go to school to learn how not to be violent shows how far man has progressed.

Many super-dooper patriots also believe in nonviolence. The only difference is that they don't believe in it quite as much as Miss Baez does. They are opposed to getting personally involved in violence and they demonstrate their opposition by scrupulously avoiding the enlistment office.

However, they do not feel as strongly about other people —such as young men of draft age—getting involved. They feel it is good for a young man's character and it helps the economy. And if the young men should get shot, the super-dooper patriots help out by providing free tickets to football games.

Another area of agreement is the income tax.

Miss Baez has a ritual she goes through in the spring. She announces publicly that she is not going to pay all of her taxes. She withholds that percentage used for war. It is one of her ways of protesting.

When this happens, the government sues her and collects the money anyway. Then they are happy because they have the money, and she is happy because she has protested.

Many of the super-patriots go through something similar to this. They hire expert lawyers who find ways they can chisel off a bit here and there. But they don't announce it. And if the lawyers are skillful, the government doesn't sue.

The anti-draft movement is another one of Miss Baez's activities. She encourages young men to duck the draft. That's part of her philosophy against violence. She believes that if young men all over the world simply refused to fight, there would be no wars. At one time this might have been true, but now, unfortunately, old men get to hold their fingers on the buttons.

Many super-dooper patriots also oppose the draft. But not completely. They oppose having junior get involved in the draft, so they foot the tuition and expenses until he is too old to go in. But they don't oppose drafting young men who can't afford campus life.

Miss Baez believes in civil rights. She has taken part in many marches and rallies and has raised funds for the movement.

The SDP's believe in civil rights. But they believe in limiting them to whites and to those Negroes who prove they are worthy. Most super-dooper patriots, however, don't know many Negroes who are worthy.

Miss Baez is against the use of LSD, glue, heroin, marijuana and all other dopes. So are most of the super-dooper patriots. Miss Baez doesn't use any of them. The super-dooper patriots say they don't, either. But when you hear them talk, you have to wonder.

Look Who's Marching Now

Something new is coming in the way of protest marches.

We are about to have a march by comfortable, white, middle-class, well-fixed, suburban kids who have nothing to complain about.

You might think that kids with nothing to complain about would have trouble finding a reason to hold a protest march.

Not at all. Today's teen-ager has great ingenuity. He talks when he has nothing to say, rushes about when he has no destination and returns after having been nowhere.

So it is perfectly natural that we should have a protest march when the marchers have no complaints.

This march will be held Saturday by about thirty or thirty-five youths from La Grange and La Grange Park, two very pretty suburbs that have median incomes above $13,000.

The organizers are calling it a "non-protest" march, but that isn't accurate.

They are really protesting against protest marches.

In their teen-age sophistication and historical ignorance, they have come to the conclusion that protest marches are a waste of time and that they do not accomplish anything.

I can understand why they would feel this way. From their suburbs, the view of the problems that cause other people to march isn't too good.

Despite the excellence of their local school systems, their view of history isn't too good, either.

Their march will not be a waste of time, they say, because they are going to have "fun and exercise." In their thick publicity packets, they rate "fun and exercise" as the finest thing a march can produce.

Their march is not going to be any short walk, I'll say that for them. They are going to hike all the way to Lake Geneva, Wisconsin, about fifty miles from their starting point.

For those who are protest-march fans, it might be interesting to compare their march plans with the more conventional type of protest march that has thrilled millions of TV viewers.

As we all know, an ordinary protest march usually features policemen, rocks, bottles and jeering crowds. The more exciting ones sometimes include people popping out of bushes with guns blazing, posses on horseback, a few cattle prods, a division or two of troops and maybe a bit of blood.

The Saturday march of the contented teens, however, is not expected to have any such ingredients.

They will be accompanied on their brave walk by adult-driven autos. The autos will be there in case any marchers suffer from blisters, fatigue or change of heart. They will also carry the marchers' beach togs.

Unless they encounter people who are enraged by the sight of teen-agers, which is always possible and understandable, they will arrive at Fox Lake for a swim and a meal.

After refreshing themselves, they will resume their march to Lake Geneva. One of them will blow a trumpet frequently to raise morale.

At Lake Geneva, adults in boats and cars will transport them to a couple of summer homes, where they will spend the night.

The next day, Sunday, they will have cookouts, swim, dance, laugh, listen to music, goof around and do all the other things that make teen-agers happy.

Then the adults will load them into cars and take them home. They will be tired, but they will have made an important point: They have nothing to complain about and therefore other people shouldn't have protest marches.

This is perfectly logical. It is like a person who is fit and healthy saying to someone who is very ill: "I feel good so stop groaning."

And they will have had fun and exercise. That is what really counts.

In fact, it could catch on among other groups. Maybe this summer they will stop marching around City Hall or into strange neighborhoods and will hike to Lake Geneva for a weekend of cookouts, swimming, laughing and whooping it up at someone's summer home. And at night, they could go home to the suburbs.

That is what the contented marchers recommend, isn't it?

COME, LET US REASON TOGETHER,
OR, SHADDAP AN' LISTEN WILLYA

Daley Dissected

Chicago is crawling with visiting writers all asking the same questions: What is Mayor Daley really like? Who is this chubby-cheeked man in City Hall who munches cookies with LBJ and is courted by Bobby? And whom will he support for the nomination?

It is a strain for local newsmen, being interviewed by visiting writers, especially the scholarly ones. They always ask if the mayor has charisma. In the mayor's neighborhood, they could get punched for talking dirty.

To assist visitors, I have prepared a primer on the mayor. Most of it isn't new to Chicagoans, but it might help others appreciate our most famous citizen.

It is needed because some visitors get confused by the many popular versions of what Mayor Daley is really like.

There is the Mayor Daley his most ardent admirers describe.

This mayor, legend has it, first appeared during the Chicago Fire of 1871. He doused the fire with one hand and milked Mrs. O'Leary's cow with the other. Before the ashes cooled, he hired Frank Lloyd Wright to redesign the city, dug Lake Michigan to cool it, organized the White Sox and set aside land for two airports in case airplanes were ever invented.

More restrained admirers say he is simply the greatest mayor Chicago ever had, which is like singling out the best player the New York Mets ever had.

The best way to view Mayor Daley is in pieces. At least that's what Republicans say.

His Early Years: The key to Daley's success is the fact he was born in a magical old neighborhood called Bridgeport. It has produced Chicago's last three mayors, their rule spanning thirty-seven years. All this political clout means nearly every family has got somebody on a government payroll. In the East, some families register a newborn son at Harvard or Yale. In Bridgeport, they sign him on with the city water department.

The mayor's father was a sheet metal worker. As a kid, Daley worked in the stockyards. This convinced him there are better things than work, so he got into politics.

He showed talent. He did what he was told, never got caught associating with newspapermen, reformers or other low types, never squealed on anybody, wore fat-Max ties, baggy suits and broad brimmed hats just like his peers and went to church on Sunday.

His only flaws were that he didn't smoke cigars or wear diamond rings, but the party overlooked this because he had been to college. During the late thirties and early forties, he served in the Legislature and came out clean, which hasn't happened too often. In the late forties, he ran for sheriff and lost. He didn't like the way that felt and it hasn't happened again.

Rise to Power: In 1955, the Democrats had a serious problem. The mayor was Martin Kennelly, a businessman and a reformer. The Democrats had put him in because there had been so much scandal they had needed a reform candidate to beat off the Republicans.

But Kennelly betrayed the Democrats by actually trying to reform things. Outraged, they dumped him for Daley, who was then the county clerk. He wasn't well known to the public, but he had power in party circles. Kennelly bravely fought Daley in the primary, but he was exposed as a reformer and the voters kicked him out.

As Mayor: Daley likes to build big things. He likes high-rises, expressways, parking garages, municipal buildings and anything else that requires a ribbon-cutting ceremony and can be financed through federal funds.

He isn't that enthusiastic about small things, such as people. Daley does not like civil rights demonstrators, rebellious community organizations, critics of the mediocre school system, critics of any kind or people who argue with him.

Daley the Public Figure: Until he became mayor, Daley was known as a quiet, behind-the-scenes politician. When he started making speeches, it was clear why he had been quiet. He has since developed two much-improved styles of oratory: a controlled mumble for TV and an excited gabble for political rallies.

He has simple tastes. Nobody catches him chatting about literature, music or French cooking. He likes White Sox games, fishing and parades. He has led more parades than anyone since Rome fell apart. Hardly a Saturday passes when the mayor isn't hoofing down the middle of State Street with thousands of city workers behind him. It has been estimated he has paraded the distance from Chicago to Minsk.

Daley the Politician: He is old-fashioned. Other city machines took up civil service and got in other bad habits. They fell apart. The old-fashioned Daley organization controls about 60,000 patronage jobs. It has thousands of others in unions, private industry, utilities, at race tracks.

Loafing or getting lost in a bar won't get a guy fired, but failing to get the vote out will. Besides patronage, the organization offers something for everyone: There are welfare checks for the obedient poor, big projects for contractors, rezoning for real estate men, prestige appointments for the socially important, promotions for the right cops and firemen.

Nepotism is big. Half the top office-holders are sons of former office-holders. Even the crime syndicate has its men in government. Everyone can join in if they do what they are told. It is truly democratic in a dictatorial sort of way.

Whom will he support for the nomination? The mayor will consider which candidate is the wisest, the noblest, the most inspiring, the best qualified. Then he will pick the one with the best chance of winning. In his parades, the politicians always march up front. No matter how pretty they sound, the flute players walk behind the horses.

Hear the One About . . .

There once was a man named George who wanted to be president.

He had a lot of what it takes: a full head of hair, a good TV image, a nice-looking wife. He was even rich and he made his pile before going into politics.

There was a war going on when George wanted to be president, so George figured he better find out what the war was all about in case someone asked him about it.

George went to the war and looked at it. He talked to the generals who were fighting the war. Then he came back and talked to the generals who were planning the war. Then he talked to the civilian thinkers who were running the generals. And he talked to the computers who were running the civilian thinkers.

All of them gave George briefings. They told him things looked good and that we were winning.

After he talked to everybody, George announced his findings:

He said he didn't know what was going on. He said he had been brainwashed.

People had never before heard a candidate say he didn't know what was going on. Even candidates who don't know what is going on don't say so.

Everybody started laughing at George. It was the funniest thing a candidate ever said.

Every day the generals and the civilians had been telling how we were winning, how many enemies we had killed, how much of the country we had freed—and here was poor George who didn't know what was going on.

Even people who hadn't gone and looked at the war, as George had, knew what was going on.

George tried to explain. He said everybody had told him lies, and that's why he was brainwashed.

But the laughter was so loud, nobody heard George anymore. They were all telling jokes about how whatever was in his brain came out in the wash, ho, ho.

As time passed, George went to that terrible place where candidates go when people laugh at them—the inside page.

The inside page is OK if you are a recipe or a death notice. But not many recipes or death notices get elected president.

The only time George ever got off the inside page and onto the front page was when somebody took a poll and found out the people weren't interested in a candidate who didn't know what was going on.

But the people George accused of washing his brain kept getting on the front page.

The generals who had told George we were winning were still saying we were winning. They said we really had the enemy on the run.

That was true. The enemy was even running into our embassy.

They said we were shooting more of the enemy than we ever had before. That was true. The enemy was even helping by coming into our territory by the thousands.

They said victory was a sure thing. And to get more people in on the victory celebration, the generals asked for 100,000 more troops.

The generals were so excited about how well things were going, that sometimes there would be two of them talking on the front page at the same time.

The general in charge of the fighting said: "I don't believe Hanoi can hold up under a long war."

And on the same day the general in charge of the planning said he saw "no early end to the war."

The Secretary of Defense went before the senators to explain why we started dropping bombs 8,000 miles away to defend ourselves.

He told all about the Tonkin Gulf incident. He had told about it 3½ years ago, but this time he changed his story.

It wasn't a big change, but just enough so some senators said they wished they had heard it that way in the first place —they would have voted differently.

And the President kept saying he wanted peace and was willing to negotiate.

So the UN said the enemy would negotiate if the President would stop bombing.

And the President who wants peace sent more bombers.

Suddenly many ordinary people, many senators, many writers said: "Hey, what the hell is going on? Has somebody been telling us lies?"

When George heard this, he brightened. He thought this was his chance to escape from the inside page. George said: "Yoo hoo! Remember me? I'm George, the one who told you about the lies in the first place."

But it was too late for George. Nobody remembered what he had told them. They just recalled that what he had said made them laugh, and this was no laughing matter.

And the people decided, as they always do, that they prefer to be led by someone who can tell a good story, rather than by someone who just knows one when he hears it.

Ronnie's Record

When I was a schoolboy dozing through U.S. history, one inspiring fact stuck in my mind. Our presidents had that old get-up-and-go right from the start. Most of them were in public life before they could grow beards.

That's probably why we've been lucky when it comes to presidents. And it has made the job of writing history textbooks easier.

Now, in the age of TV and campaign managers who are smarter than their candidates, there exists the genuine possibility that Ronald Reagan will become president.

It might be interesting to see how his career to date looks when compared with those of the men who have held the highest office.

Let's start with the years heading to manhood, the getting-started years—zero to 25.

At 14, Andrew Jackson was taken prisoner by the British and was slashed with a sword because he wouldn't shine an officer's boots.

By the time they were 25, Teddy Roosevelt, James Buchanan, John Tyler, Franklin Pierce, James Monroe, Abe Lincoln and others were state legislators.

George Washington was a colonel, John Tyler a congressman and Herbert Hoover was running all over the Far East building mines.

Ronald wasn't marking time. At 25 he was a sports announcer in Des Moines, Iowa. "Dutch" Reagan, they called him. He had gone into radio after finishing at Eureka College. His most notable public service had been as a lifeguard at resorts during school vacations.

Thirty is one of those milestone birthdays.

At that age Polk, Madison, JFK and LBJ were congressmen. Taft was a state judge. Teddy Roosevelt had been beaten for mayor of New York, but at 31 he was on the U.S. Civil Service Commission. Martin Van Buren and FDR

121

were state senators. Garfield was a Union Army general at 31. Jefferson and his friends were stirring up trouble for England.

Ronald was moving right along.

He took a screen test. Des Moines's loss was Hollywood's gain. His first movie, at 27, was *Love Is on the Air*. He played a radio announcer.

Before he was 30, America thrilled to *Brother Rat, Boy Meets Girl, Going Places, Naughty but Nice, Angels Wash Their Faces, Angel from Texas, Murder in the Air* and many others.

Critics hailed him as being mediocre.

He was photographed changing trains.

He married Jane Wyman and they had a baby.

But at 31, Ronald put the baby down, kissed Jane good-by and marched off to war. He spent World War II as an officer, making training films. The Army loaned him to Hollywood for a while so he could appear in a war movie. George Murphy, now a senator, played his father.

Meanwhile, back in history, the future presidents were hustling through their busy 30's.

Andrew Jackson made it to the Senate at 32, Pierce and Monroe at 33 and Kennedy at 36. Van Buren was New York's attorney general at 34. Lincoln got to Congress at 37, Madison at 38. Taft was a federal judge at 35. Teddy Roosevelt charged up San Juan Hill at 38.

Even Harry Truman, a notably late starter, was a county commissioner in Missouri at 38. Herbert Hoover was considered one of the world's great engineers and was a millionaire before 40.

And Thomas Jefferson wrote the Declaration of Independence when he was 33.

Ronald wasn't exactly goofing off. In a landslide vote, he was elected head of the Hollywood actors' union. And he was only 37.

By then he had starred in *Stallion Road, That Hagen Girl* and the *Voice of the Turtle*.

People read about him. One story told how he used his own personal red and white striped pajamas in a movie scene.

Politics entered the scene. Jane Wyman, in divorcing him, revealed that they had differing political views but he didn't think hers were important.

A man with a future really flexes his career-muscles in his 40's.

At 42, Teddy Roosevelt was president, Jefferson (he always had something going) was minister to France, Rutherford Hayes was governor of Ohio, LBJ was a senator.

At 43, Kennedy was president, Washington was running the Continental Army, Hoover was head of the U.S. Food Administration.

In their mid-40's, Grant was president, FDR and Grover Cleveland were governors, Jefferson was secretary of state, Gen. Andrew Jackson whipped the British in New Orleans, Hoover was secretary of commerce, Woodrow Wilson was running Princeton and most of the others had an iron or two in the fire.

And Ronald, at 40, was co-starring with a monkey. The critics gave Bonzo (*Bed Time for Bonzo*) the better of the reviews.

About this time, Ronald stopped being a liberal and became a conservative. (Most presidents made up their minds a bit earlier.) And this was when he remarried. His wife was a member of a socially prominent and politically conservative Chicago family.

And the press quoted him as saying that Hollywood was being infiltrated by the Reds.

By the time he was 46 or so, he was soaring toward collision with history.

He took a firm public stand against critics of Hollywood marriages. He lashed out against the "sweatshirt school of acting." He acted on TV and became a goodwill ambassador for his sponsor, General Electric.

Displaying Jeffersonian versatility, he made more movies and found time to boast that those Reds had finally been driven out of Hollywood.

Their 50's were the years when most presidents made it. All but seven were in the White House before their 60th birthdays. And in his 50's, Eisenhower had a pound of stars on his shoulders.

When he was 50, Ronald revealed that those Hollywood Reds weren't whipped after all—they were back again.

Now a staunch conservative, he was lecturing GE employees on the perils of creeping socialism, federal aid to schools, Social Security and the Tennessee Valley Authority.

Bonzo the chimp faded away, never having run for public office.

Finally, at age 55, Ronald ran for office. And California being the world's largest outdoor asylum, he became a governor.

Now his supporters, with all the rudeness of consumptives who won't cover their mouths when they cough, want to share Ronald with the entire country. They want him to take his place in history.

If it happens, historians will have an easier time writing it than future generations will have in reading it. Those caves get awfully dark.

He Deserved Better

There were those who screamed with a vicious joy when President Johnson, in that slow, sad way of his, said he is not running again.

There were others who reacted with sullen cynicism, asking what his angle is.

The white racists said "good." The black racists said "good." The super-hawks said good and the doves said good. And most of all, the young said good.

They were all so busy being jubilant in this strong man's terrible moment that many didn't listen to the serious thing he told them.

The President of the United States told the people of the United States they are so divided against themselves he dares not take part in a political campaign for fear that it could get even worse.

But they answered, many of them, with one last jeer of contempt and hatred.

It figured. Unrestrained hatred has become the dominant emotion in this splintered country. Races hate, age groups hate, political extremes hate. And when they aren't hating each other, they have been turning it on LBJ. He, more than anyone else, has felt it.

The white racists, those profoundly ignorant broads who toss eggs at school buses, blamed him for the very existence of the Negro. To them he was a "nigger lover."

The black separatists could find no insult too vile to be used on him. To them he was a white racist. That he launched some of the most ambitious civil rights legislation in the nation's history means nothing in a time when black scholars say Abe Lincoln was the worst kind of bigot.

The super-hawks complained that he wasn't killing the VC fast enough.

The doves portrayed him as engaging in war almost for the fun of it.

And the young, that very special group, were offended by him in so many, many ways.

For one thing, he was old. They might have forgiven him that if he had at least acted young. But he acted like a harassed, tremendously busy, impatient man with an enormous responsibility. Just like their old man.

He offended them by failing to pander to them, by not fawning over them and telling them that they were the wise ones, that they had the answers, that they could guide us. He didn't tell them that because he was the man charged with running the country, not them.

He offended others by engaging in an "unjust" war. Their collective conscience rebelled against the "unjust" war. So they portrayed him as the eager murderer of babies. Just how many of these conscience-tormented young men are more tormented by the thought of being rousted out of bed at 5 A.M. by a drill sergeant than by the thought of a burned village, we'll never know.

And he offended many by his lack of style and wit, his sore-footed hound dog oratory.

So the abuse he took from all was remarkable. Presidents, like all politicians, have to take abuse. It is within the rules of the game to criticize them, to spoof them, to assail them.

But there may not have been anything in our history to compare with what has been tossed at President Johnson in the last four years.

A play that says he arranged the murder of John F. Kennedy has been a hit with the intellectuals, and those who think they are.

A somewhat popular publication of satire called *The Realist* printed something so obscene about him that I can't find a way to even hint at it.

High government officials were hooted down when they tried to represent the administration point of view on campuses, those temples of free speech.

Every smart punk grabbed a sign and accused him of being in a class with Hitler or Richard Speck. The nation's nuts vowed to come to Chicago during the convention and turn it into anything from an outdoor orgy to a historic riot as their contribution to the democratic process.

He needed more personal protection than any president in history. That can't feel very good. But it was necessary. We have people who burn cities and many others who go to movies and howl with glee at the violent scenes.

If you live in a big city, you see the hate that threatens it. He lived in the whole country and looked at it all. And he couldn't see a way to unite it.

Maybe he wasn't the best president we might have had.

But we sure as hell aren't the best people a president has ever had.

Praise the Lord and Pass the Ammunition

Maybe it's time to change the words to our song to bring it up-to-date and capture the national spirit:

Oh, say can you see by the pawnshop's dim light
What a swell .38 with its pearl handle gleaming.
In a gun catalog is a telescope sight;
I'll send for it quick, while the sirens are screaming.
And the TV's white glare, the shots ripping in air
Give proof through the night that our guns are still
*   there.*
Oh, don't you ever try to take my guns away from me
Because the right to shoot at you is what I mean by
*   liberty.*

And why not? We should glorify the gun. It is our national symbol. Who owns an eagle? How many of us have ever seen an eagle? But guns—we have 100,000,000 of them in private circulation. Maybe there are as many Bibles around as guns, but their impact doesn't show.

This country has so many guns because guns are very useful. I know this to be the truth because the gun-lovers and their lobbyists, such as the National Rifle Association, tell us so.

They tell us that guns are good for fighting crime.

If you have a gun in your house, you can shoot a burglar. Of course, the burglar can buy a gun, too, so maybe he will shoot you.

Or, he might break into your home when you aren't there and steal your gun. Then he can use it to shoot a storekeeper and a cop. But they might arrest him, so the net result would be one storekeeper and one cop shot, and a burglar in jail.

The gun is so effective as a crime-fighting device that the United States, with more privately owned guns than any other country, has the highest crime rate in the world.

What I've never understood, though, is why people can

legally own rifles, shotguns or pistols, but can't own other fine anti-crime weapons.

Why can't I own a machine gun? I'm not much of a shot with a pistol, but I'm sure I could wing a burglar with a machine gun.

In fact, I'd like to buy a surplus tank from the Army—fully activated, of course.

I want a tank because the gun people say we might have to fight off foreign invaders some day. Apparently our Army, Navy, Air Force, Marines and nuclear stockpile aren't up to the job.

If that's so, I'd feel more comfortable in a tank with my cannon blazing.

While waiting for the invasion, I could put it to home use. There isn't much difference between a tank and the legal guns. You aren't any less dead when struck by a tank shell than a shotgun blast.

Grenades should be legal, too. A fellow could knock out an entire burglary gang with one grenade. Yet, a grenade isn't any more lethal than a cheap mail-order rifle. You can't kill a president at two hundred yards with a grenade, even if you have a strong arm.

Gun-lovers instruct us that our right to build private arsenals is guaranteed by the Second Amendment of the Constitution.

That's the one gun-lovers always quote this way: "The right of the people to keep and bear arms shall not be infringed."

Actually, it doesn't say just that. The entire sentence is: "A well regulated militia being necessary to the security of a free state, the right of the people to keep and bear arms shall not be infringed."

So gun-lovers interpret this to mean that in order to have a well-regulated militia, anybody should be able to own guns. Not having graduated from West Point, I don't know if that is entirely true. It does seem like a strange way to build a militia.

But if they look at it that way, they should do something to help the dope fiend.

We all know that morphine can be a useful pain-reliever. Yet you can't buy it in the drugstore.

It seems reasonable that if guns should be sold to almost anybody in order to build a state militia, morphine should be sold to almost anybody to help those in pain.

And what about that part of the Constitution that guarantees our right "to pursuit of happiness." Many people find their happiness in marijuana or LSD, but the cops pursue them while they pursue their happiness.

Tradition is a big factor in gun ownership. Americans used guns to shoot Indians, the British, wild turkeys and buffalo, Mexicans and each other.

It's no longer necessary for us to shoot Indians, the British, wild turkeys and buffalo, Mexicans and each other, but we still own the guns. Tradition.

I believe in tradition. So I consider the Health Department to be un-American.

An even older tradition than gun ownership is the right to keep pigs, chickens, goats and cattle in your back yard.

But they won't let me.

Everybody should be able to keep pigs, chickens, goats and cattle in their back yards. Or in their high-rise apartments. Or in their office lobbies.

That way, if the Communists ever take over all the farms and meat-packing houses and try to starve us to death (they won't dare shoot it out because of our guns), we will be well stocked with our own food supply.

I'd write more about our precious right to bear arms, but I've got to go to a meeting of a committee to replace the torch in the Statue of Liberty's hand with a .22 pistol.

So if you want to fight for your right to own guns, cut this column out and send it to your congressman or your senator.

Quick, while they are still alive.

SO WHAT'S NEW?

Chicago Mourns . . . but Not Too Much

The country mourned over the weekend. People looked into their hearts.

This is what it is like in Chicago when people go into mourning and look into their hearts.

It was hot Saturday night, so Nathan Ross and his sister walked to the lake. On the way back, they stopped to rest. Ross has deformed feet and he's fifty-eight, so he tires easily.

While they were sitting on a front porch on Lawrence Avenue, a man ran up to Ross. His sister says she doesn't know who he was or why he did it. The man shot Ross in the head and killed him. Then he ran away. Just like that.

Maurice Lee, twenty-six, took a walk, too. He was walking with his wife when a gang of kids jumped him. He struggled, and one of them shot him in the head. Mrs. Lee went home a widow.

A man stood in front of a judge and was told he must never hit his son that hard again or next time he'd go to jail. The nine-year-old boy had stolen a can of shoe polish. His father taught him right from wrong by splitting his head so it took ten stitches to close and by whipping open cuts in his back.

LaMar McCoy figured that if Bonnie and Clyde and Jesse James could do it, he could do it. He got a gun and went looking for money, just like a folk hero.

He went in a restaurant and drew on a woman cashier. She pulled out a gun and shot him in the head. She was lucky. Sometimes the robber is shot. More often, the storekeeper is. But with millions of guns around, the battle never ends.

Thomas Daniel, a gas station attendant, was just cleaning his gun. The doctors say he will survive despite the large hole it made in his abdomen.

In the case of Guy Bibbs, somebody insulted somebody

else in a tavern on Pulaski Road. The details will all come out later when an inquest is held into Bibbs's death.

Abder Rayyan wasn't bothering anybody. He was in his grocery store when two men came in and shot him in the head. The police figure they were mad at him because he's a Jordanian and it was their way of avenging Senator Kennedy's death. Just like in the better westerns they have probably seen.

And somebody broke into Mrs. Sophie McElvenny's apartment on Lake Shore Drive and strangled her. She was a widow and a cripple.

John Hicks was quarreling with a friend over how to raise dogs. The friend finally settled the argument by stabbing Hicks in the heart.

Jim McPherson was stabbed eleven times, but he was lucky enough to survive. As far as anyone can tell, he was just walking near the lake on the Far North Side when half a dozen large young men felt like killing him.

At about the same hour, the County Morgue got the bodies of a man named Driver and a woman named Young. They didn't know each other and had nothing in common, except their respective mates had stabbed them to death during domestic quarrels. It is cheaper, in the long run, to hire divorce lawyers.

In a park in the suburb of Chicago Heights, some teenagers got angry about something. Insults, the police say. Scott Cross died at the age of eighteen of a knife wound.

If she's lucky Margaret White will live. The police came by her street just in time to grab the man who was standing over her with a bloody brick in his hand.

By police standards, it was a fairly quiet weekend in Chicago.

There were only five murders with guns, and three or four with knives, plus a strangulation.

Of course, there were hundreds of other people put into hospitals by fists and feet, bottles and bats.

There were the assaults on the nervous systems. People

on North Burling couldn't sleep much after some punks tossed homemade bombs on their porches, shattering dozens of windows. Nobody knows why. Just for fun, probably.

There were the wife beaters and children beaters, the street-corner brawls, the dozens of people who settled quarrels by slugging someone else.

We can't even begin to list all of those. I'm paid to write a daily column, not a daily book.

Mary and Joe, Chicago-Style

Mary and Joe were flat broke when they got off the bus in Chicago. They didn't know anybody and she was expecting a baby.

They went to a cheap hotel. But the clerk jerked his thumb at the door when they couldn't show a day's rent in advance.

They walked the streets until they saw a police station. The desk sergeant said they couldn't sleep in a cell, but he told them how to get to the Cook County Department of Public Aid.

A man there said they couldn't get regular assistance because they hadn't been Illinois residents long enough. But he gave them the address of the emergency welfare office on the West Side.

It was a two-mile walk up Madison Street to 19 S. Damen. Someone gave them a card with a number on it and they sat down on a bench, stared at the peeling green paint and waited for their number to be called.

Two hours later, a caseworker motioned them forward, took out blank forms and asked questions: Any relatives? Any means of getting money? Any assets?

Joe said he owned a donkey. The caseworker told him not to get smart or he'd be thrown out. Joe said he was sorry.

The caseworker finished the forms and said they were entitled to emergency CTA fare to County Hospital because of Mary's condition. And he told Joe to go to an Urban Progress Center for occupational guidance.

Joe thanked him and they took a bus to the hospital. A guard told them to wait on a bench. They waited two hours, then Mary got pains and they took her away. Someone told Joe to come back tomorrow.

He went outside and asked a stranger on the street for directions to an Urban Progress Center. The stranger hit Joe on the head and took his overcoat. Joe was still lying there when a paddy wagon came along so they pinched him for being drunk on the street.

Mary had a baby boy during the night. She didn't know it, but three foreign-looking men in strange, colorful robes came to the hospital asking about her and the baby. A guard took them for hippies and called the police. They found odd spices on the men so the narcotics detail took them downtown for further questioning.

The next day Mary awoke in a crowded ward. She asked for Joe. Instead, a representative of the Planned Parenthood Committee came by to give her a lecture on birth control.

Next, a social worker came for her case history. She asked Mary who the father was. Mary answered and the social worker ran for the nurse. The nurse questioned her and Mary answered. The nurse stared at her and ran for the doctor. The doctor wrote "Post partum delusion" on her chart.

An ambulance took Mary to the Cook County Mental Health Clinic the next morning. A psychiatrist asked her questions and pursed his lips at the answers.

A hearing was held and a magistrate committed her to the Chicago State Hospital, Irving Park and Narragansett.

Joe got out of the House of Correction a couple of days later and went to the County Hospital for Mary. They told him she was at Chicago State and the baby had been placed in a foster home by the State Department of Children and Family Services.

When Joe got to Chicago State, a doctor told him what Mary had said about the baby's birth. Joe said Mary was telling the truth. They put Joe in a ward at the other end of the hospital.

Meanwhile, the three strangely dressed foreign-looking men were released after the narcotics detail could find no laws prohibiting the possession of myrrh and frankincense. They returned to the hospital and were taken for civil rights

demonstrators. They were held in the County Jail on $100,-
000 bond.

By luck, Joe and Mary met on the hospital grounds. They
decided to tell the doctors what they wanted to hear. The
next day they were declared sane and were released.

When they applied for custody of Mary's baby, however,
they were told it was necessary for them to first establish
a proper residence, earn a proper income and create a suit-
able environment.

They applied at the Urban Progress Center for training
under the Manpower Development Program. Joe said he
was good at working with wood. He was assigned to a
computer data-processing class. Mary said she'd gladly do
domestic work. She was assigned to a course in key-punch
operating. Both got $20-a-week stipends.

Several months later they finished the training. Joe got
a job in a gas station and Mary went to work as a waitress.

They saved their money and hired a lawyer. Another custody hearing was held and several days later the baby was
ordered returned to them.

Reunited finally, they got back to their two-room flat and
met the landlord on the steps. He told them Urban Renewal
had ordered the building torn down. The City Relocation
Bureau would get them another place.

They packed, dressed the baby and hurried to the Grey-
hound bus station.

Joe asked the ticket man when the next bus was leaving.

"Where to?" the ticket man asked.

"Anywhere," Joe said, "as long as it is right now."

He gave Joe three tickets and in five minutes they were
on a bus heading for southern Illinois—the area known as
"Little Egypt."

Just as the bus pulled out, the three strangely dressed
men ran into the station. But they were too late. It was gone.

So they started hiking down U.S. 66. But at last report
they were pinched on suspicion of being foreigners in il-
legal possession of gold.

Poverty, Who Can Afford It?

Just for fun, let's go food shopping with a rich lady from the North Shore and a poor ADC mama from the Taylor Homes.

They'll use the same shopping list, but they won't shop in the same store.

The rich lady will drive over to a supermarket near the Old Orchard shopping center, Skokie.

The poor lady will walk over to a supermarket on S. State Street.

This is the shopping list I've prepared for them. No fancy frills; just basics.

One dozen eggs, a pound of butter, two pounds of coffee, four cans of chicken noodle soup, two cans of frozen orange juice, three cans of spinach, three cans of green beans, two cans of peas, a pound of pork chops, two pounds of ground beef, a bottle of catsup, five pounds of flour, a pound package of bologna, a pound of tomatoes, a pint of salad dressing, a pound of hot dogs.

Except for the meats, the products are identical brand names.

The rich lady shopping on the North Shore will pay $9.92.

The lady from Taylor Homes shopping on S. State will pay $11.63.

Admittedly, this would not be a typical shopping list for women from either economic class. But it illustrates the high cost of being poor.

The only products in the list cheaper at the S. State Street store are tomatoes, hot dogs and ground beef.

The others range from a few pennies difference (Campbell's chicken noodle soup, 19 cents to 16 cents) to a substantial price spread (Maxwell House coffee, $1.79 to $1.22 for two pounds).

Catsup costs the ADC mama 29 cents. The same brand costs her North Shore counterpart 24 cents.

Frozen orange juice is 29 cents for a relief recipient in the Taylor Homes. The same six-ounce can costs the lady with a maid 15 cents.

If the above prices are representative, the person who can least afford it is spending something like 15 to 20 per cent more for the same food products.

And that is often a person on relief who is allotted about 17 cents a person per meal.

The S. State Street store—one of a small chain operating in poor Negro areas—says it is just following standard prices. A spokesman asserted that meat prices at the S. State Street store are cheaper than at most other stores. However, meat prices are difficult to compare because of differences in grades.

William Robinson, director of Cook County Public Aid, said the high cost of food in low-income Negro neighborhoods is almost a tradition. "It is my understanding that they are almost always higher," he said.

Ironically, middle-class Negroes only a couple of miles from Taylor Homes are paying substantially less for their food.

At a store operated in the Lake Meadows high-rise area, food prices are noticeably lower than in the S. State Street store.

Even grits, not found in most white shopping areas, cost the Lake Meadows Negro less—39 cents to 49 cents for a large sack.

A home economist for the public aid department said the low-income Negro is trapped by high food prices.

"If a white person in Chicago or a suburb knows that she is paying high prices, she can go somewhere else. She probably has a car or her husband drives her.

"But the very poor—and that's what these people are—must go where they can walk and where they can carry what they buy.

"We know this is happening, that they are paying much higher prices for food—often for inferior products—but there is nothing we can do except try to educate them on wiser shopping.

"That's why you'll often see Negro domestics who work in the North Shore buying food in the stores up there and bringing it home on the L. They can save a few dollars a week that way.

"About the only thing that can bring prices down in those areas is competition. Merchants don't seem to give an inch on their own."

I can't help but suspect that there is some relationship between the cost of catsup in the winter and the cost of replacing busted store windows in the summer.

A "Natural" Death

The day they held an inquest into Rosie Stewart's death, the coroner's office didn't bother to notify anyone. They didn't tell her mother, her sister, her boyfriend, the doctor and nurse at County Hospital, the paddy wagon men, the firemen, nobody.

The rules say the family, at least, ought to be notified about an inquest. But the coroner's man said it wouldn't have mattered.

"A case like hers," said the sleek, political-type assistant coroner, "what's the point in having witnesses and taking testimony? No matter what anybody says, the verdict is going to be that she died a natural death, so why waste time?"

What is a "natural" death? In Rose Stewart's case, the records say she died of something called myrocardia. It is a heart ailment. She was nineteen.

And that means it was nobody's fault. That is why the coroner's office couldn't get interested. If someone had hit Rosie on the head with a rock, it would have been different. They would have called witnesses, probably, and held an inquiry. But they say her death was "natural."

This is what her "natural" death looked like through the eyes of her boyfriend, John Pinkerton, 19, a Crane High School senior.

"She started feeling sick on Sunday. She said she felt sick all over and she had pain in her side. On Monday she could hardly stand up she was so weak, so I took her to County.

"I thought they'd put her in a bed and treat her. But after they examined her, a woman, the nurse, said she could go home. I asked them why they wouldn't keep her there and they said she wasn't that sick.

"They gave me a prescription for her to fill out so I went to the front lobby where they fill them and I put her on a bench to wait.

"The lady there said she couldn't fill it. By the time I got back to Rosie, she'd passed out on the floor. A couple of guards were taking her back to be looked at again.

"They had her in a room there for about an hour. Then a doctor came out and asked who was with her. He told me they gave her a couple of shots. He said one of them would relax her. I don't know what the other was. They said I could take her home and if she didn't feel good to have her take a warm bath.

"She could still hardly stand up, but I got her in a cab and took her to my house where me and my mother could look after her.

"Later in the evening she started breathing real hard, panting sort of. We did like they said. We put her in the warm bath. My mother sat in the bathroom with her.

"I was in the parlor when my mother started screaming. Rosie had passed out in the tub. We got her out and sat her up, but she didn't open her eyes again. The firemen came and gave her oxygen, but she was dead. So they took her back to the County Hospital to have someone there pronounce her dead."

After that, it was the County Morgue, where a pathologist studied her organs and determined that her heart had given out—her death, "natural."

One day last week, Dr. Karl Meyer, the 81-year-old medical superintendent of all county institutions, including the hospital, sat looking at a pink card with some words scribbled on it.

He's been looking at such cards since 1914, when he first became the hospital's medical superintendent. The words on the card told about Rosie's last visit.

"Well, let's see . . . she had sickle cell anemia," he finally said. This is an anemia peculiar to Negroes. Those who have it don't get malaria. It makes a person feel weak, they have pains in their abdomen, but a person can live with it. "We give them blood," Dr. Meyer said.

He studied the pink card further. He murmured: "She

had been treated here in the past for jaundice. See, it says right here, a notation about her color. Her temperature was 98.2.

"Penicillin. They gave her a shot of penicillin. No, it wouldn't help the anemia. They wouldn't give it to her for that. They probably gave it to her in case she had an infection.

"Let's see, anything else? No, I don't see anything else here. I guess not. Penicillin, that's all."

He put the card down.

"Things like this can happen. Yes, people can walk out of their family doctor's office after a complete physical and drop dead of a heart attack. Why, that happened to, let's see, was it Ed Kelly? Yes, Mayor Kelly. He walked out of his doctor's office feeling fine. Then he dropped dead."

But Rosie Stewart was feeling less than fine when she left the County. She could hardly walk.

"Yes, but there's the problem of space. We have a lot of people coming here. If we put her in a bed out in a hallway, why, we'd be criticized for that."

He picked up the pink card again and looked at it.

"Remember, I've told these young fellows, if there's doubt, put them in a bed. I've always said that. But things like this happen.

"It can happen anywhere. A person can walk out of his doctor's office and have a heart attack. There was a mayor of Chicago—Ed Kelly, wasn't it? Yes, Kelly, he walked out . . ."

The Last to Know

A man came and took Mrs. Rosie Davis's phone out of her apartment recently. When she asked him why, he told her "orders." That's why most people do what they do to each other today, but Rosie wanted to know more.

She went to the phone company office and asked a girl behind a counter why they took her phone. The girl checked the files and gave Rosie some very bad news. She said Rosie is dead. The phone company doesn't give phones to the dead. They can't make money that way.

Rosie went home and crawled in bed. It was the worst news she's had in a long time. She knew she was in bad shape, what with arthritis, diabetes and an unreliable heart. But this was the first hint she had that she was completely gone.

Later, though, she got to thinking about how she could still move her arms and legs, and she decided they had to be wrong. They're pretty sharp at the phone company, but medicine isn't their racket. Rosie told somebody about it and they said she looked alive. They told me and I've checked and there's no question—Rosie is alive. As she put it, in a very logical way:

"How could I be talkin' to you if I'm dead?"

Rosie's trouble is that she is a 58-year-old widow, in bad health and broke, and she has fallen into the clutches of the social workers. When the social workers get you, you might as well be dead. They'll soon have you feeling that way.

It was the social workers from the welfare office who told the phone company that Rosie had died. None of them admits it, but one of them did it.

Rosie is on welfare and the social workers don't think she needs a phone. A phone is considered a luxury item for someone on welfare and only the most needy get them.

They let Rosie have one for a while because she was sick.

She says she is still sick. When you are sick, welfare gives you a phone because you might have to call a doctor.

But the welfare people say Rosie used the phone too much. She called her daughter and a few friends and talked more than three minutes. This ran the bill up. Some months it was three or four dollars higher than it should have been. You'd think Rosie was a suburban teen-ager.

As one social worker put it: "She was using the phone for social reasons."

Rosie admits it. She pleads guilty to using the phone for "social reasons." Her age and her ailments prevent her from making the scene at discotheques, Fritzel's or ski lodges. She lives alone in a public housing apartment. So Rosie admits that she has been using the phone for "social reasons." It beats talking to the TV set or the coffee pot all day.

The social workers let her get away with it for a while. When the bill exceeded $4.20 a month (the maximum she's allowed), they'd deduct the extra cost from the check that provides her food, clothing, etc. So, in effect, Rosie was paying for her wild "social" life by sacrificing something else.

Rosie said she didn't mind, but it bothered somebody at welfare, and they finally had her phone yanked.

Now, when she gets feeling social, she has only to go downstairs and walk about 100 yards to an outdoor public phone, which ought to enliven her social life when the first snowfall hits.

But as a social worker put it: "We felt it was for Mrs. Davis's best interest that the phone service be discontinued. We can't allow herself to jeopardize her health."

Social workers know all about such things, but my guess is that an old lady's health might go a little faster if she is cooped up and lonely too long.

The least they could do, though, is tell someone when they are dead. You shouldn't have to get such bad news from the phone company.

And they should let the phone remain for a day or two. It's bad enough hearing you are dead without being unable to phone a relative so they can weep and send flowers.

Now You See It . . .

Ance Binkley figured he was on the wrong street. It had to be the wrong street because his building was supposed to be where that vacant lot was.

He drove to the corner and looked at the street sign. It was the street, all right—Giles Avenue. He went back and checked the address. It should have been the right address. That's when he realized his building was gone.

The city had struck again. It's almost like sleight of hand. Here you own a building. Presto! Now you own a vacant lot.

As is usually the case, the city had intended to notify Mr. Binkley. But it kept tripping over its own feet.

First, there was the building department. It decided the vacant building was dangerous and should be repaired or torn down.

Before it can be torn down, the owner must be warned and given a chance to repair it.

The building department sent a letter—to the owner of the vacant lot next to Mr. Binkley's building.

When the building department didn't hear from Mr. Binkley, who hadn't heard from the building department, the building department took the logical next step: the city's lawyers asked for a court order to demolish the building.

Before a judge can issue such an order, the owner has to have his day in court. Or at least he should be given a chance to come to court.

The city attorney's office set out to find the owners of Mr. Binkley's property—in other words, Mr. Binkley or the man who holds the mortgage on it.

Mr. Binkley should not have been hard to find. He is listed in the tax books as the guy who pays the taxes for the building, and his address is there. But nobody contacted him.

Instead, the city tried to contact Alan Edelson, who holds the mortgage on the building.

A process server from the sheriff's office found Alan Edelson living in an apartment on Lake Shore Drive.

The trouble is, he was the wrong Edelson. As he says: "I have been pestered to hell with summonses. I don't know anything about that building."

The sheriff's process server did not contact Alan Edelson of Glencoe, who is the right Alan Edelson. Apparently Sheriff Woods's office has never heard of the suburban phone book.

Having failed to serve a summons on Mr. Binkley or Mr. Edelson, the city took the next step required by law: it published its intention to demolish the building in a newspaper.

It published it six times, in fact. It was really in there trying.

But the officials made one mistake. They published the fact that they were going to demolish the building at the address next door—the vacant lot.

Having then failed to find Mr. Binkley, who was in the tax rolls, and having chased the wrong Mr. Edelson, and having announced they were going to demolish a vacant lot—the city tore down Binkley's building.

I am happy to report that the wrecking crew did not pull the roof down on their own heads.

I think I know why the city makes mistakes such as these, or those they made in the case of Ed Bak, the Northwest Side hardware operator who lost a pretty good building on Division Street.

In his last campaign, Mayor Daley vowed that all structurally dangerous buildings would be gone from Chicago by the end of 1967.

The year 1967 is gone, but the dangerous buildings aren't.

The mayor shouldn't be criticized for this because campaign promises are like the promises young men make to young ladies during courtship.

But the building department and the city lawyers were

so frantic to make the mayor's promise come true, they started acting like tornadoes.

They are still at it, making Chicago a wrecking company's dream.

Knocking down dangerous buildings is fine. But the city should observe the legal niceties.

When the city knocks down a bad building and the owner has his day in court, he suffers the loss, as he should for letting it deteriorate.

But when the city doesn't give him his legal rights, he can get a chunk of money if he goes to court, as Mr. Binkley has done. And tax money shouldn't be used to reward slum owners for their neglect.

Maybe the mayor should tell his people that he appreciates their efforts to make his campaign oratory come true, but to stop acting like this is Georgia and they are General Sherman's troops.

Until then, be prepared for anything, such as nothing, when you get home at night.

And be thankful the building department doesn't have The Bomb.

Loafers of the World, Unite!

Social workers are being sent into Chicago pool halls for the malicious purpose of pursuading pool players to take regular jobs.

This is part of the federal war on poverty and it shows how dirty a war—even a poverty war—can be.

As a taxpayer I object to my money being used for such an inhuman purpose. Napalm bombs on villages are one thing. How can we make Vietnam free if we don't first burn it? But infiltrating pool halls with social workers is an atrocity.

Pool halls have always been off limits to certain types of undesirables, such as women, children and preachers, and that is as it should be. The pool hall provides a sanctuary for men who want to escape creeping togetherness, one of the great dangers to our way of life.

Few such sanctuaries remain. Bowling alleys used to be almost as good as pool halls. Some of the most stimulating conversation ever heard occurred when a wine-loving pinsetter and a beer-drinking bowler argued about whether the bowler intentionally threw a ball while the pinsetter's head was in the way. But now the bowling alley has become a family center. Instead of sending their children outside to play in the fresh air pollution, parents send them to kiddy bowling leagues before they are even old enough to falsify their ID's.

Taverns long ago adopted the bad practice of admitting women, which led to the wall signs that prohibit swearing and other simple pleasures.

The pool hall alone has tried to retain its dignity and traditions. It's been difficult because of the emergence of the psuedo-pool hall, places that actually encourage women and families to enter and play. These are not really pool halls. They are simply public basement recreation rooms.

So the pool hall has slowly dwindled in number. Only a few good ones remain in Chicago—simple, quiet places where men can gather to swear, lie, shoot pool or watch someone else shoot pool, hustle or be hustled, read a scratch sheet, bet, doze, all without intrusion.

There is nothing like a pool hall, except maybe a steam bath, and there is not much to bet on in a steam bath.

The few remaining pool halls won't survive if social workers start coming around and bothering the players about going to work.

I don't even trust the motives of the social workers. Do they actually believe that pool players do not know that there are jobs available outside of the pool hall? Of course they know it. It was the thought of working regularly that sent so many of them into the pool hall in the first place.

As the great Rudolph Wanderone, better known as Minnesota Fats, has often said on the subject of work:

"I ain't never lifted anything heavier than a fork, and I never will."

Or as the lesser-known Slats Grobnik, also known as Armitage Avenue Stupid, has often said:

"If work is so good, how come we got rid of the twelve-hour day?"

Fats would not have become a great pool player, thereby avoiding regular work, if a Miss Sally Dewgood had been popping out of the corner pocket and nagging him about filling out a welfare form or taking a job in a bakery. His nerves would have been ruined and America would have lost a great athlete and an inspiration to youth.

I suspect that the social workers really don't care if pool players work. They are offended by the thought of happy, shiftless men surviving without their help. They want to inject them with ambition, upward mobility, stability and other dread social diseases.

An American institution is in danger and the social workers should be stopped. We might not save the lake, but we can save the pool player.

Remember, there are 75,000,000 people holding jobs in the United States. But there is only one Minnesota Fats.

SWEET MYSTERY OF LIFE

Down at Credibility Gap

"Grandpa, I found an old book in the closet and there's a funny word in it that I don't understand."

"Which word, sonny?"

"Here, grandpa, that one."

"Well, I'll be darned. I haven't seen that word in years and years."

"What does it mean, grandpa: L-I-A-R."

"It means someone who tells lies, sonny."

"Lies? What does that mean, telling lies?"

"It's a long story, sonny, from a long time ago."

"Goody, grandpa, I like stories about the olden days. Tell me."

"Well, once upon a time, people used the word 'liar.' If someone said something that wasn't true, and he knew it wasn't true, he was called a 'liar.' And the untrue thing was called a 'lie.'

"Then one day in the city of Washington something strange happened.

"A newspaper correspondent got to thinking about how the president wasn't telling him the truth about a war we were having and some other things. And he thought that the president's helpers weren't telling the truth, either.

"So he sat at his typewriter and tried to write about the lies.

"But he didn't know how to say it. You see, he'd been in Washington so long he'd forgotten he was a newspaperman. He thought he was a gentleman."

"But what's the difference, grandpa?"

"Big difference, sonny. If there's a big puddle in the street, a gentleman puts his coat down for a lady to walk on. But a newspaperman spits in the puddle, then goes and asks the sewer department why the puddle isn't draining."

"Then what happened, grandpa?"

155

"The Washington correspondent thought and thought about how to say everybody was lying without hurting their feelings so there wouldn't be any friction at the next cocktail party.

"And finally he got an idea. Instead of saying anything about lies, he coined the phrase, 'Credibility gap.'

"The next day people read it and got excited. They said: 'My, did you read that there is a credibility gap in Washington?' 'Oh, how nice. We will go and see it on our next vacation.'

"And from that day forward, nobody in Washington got accused of telling lies or was called a liar. Instead, their credibility was questionable or there was a gap in it."

"Did the politicans like that, grandpa?"

"Loved it, sonny. Politicians never did like calling each other liars because then they were finally telling the truth. And in politics, nothing hurts like the truth."

"What did the people think, grandpa?"

"As usual, not much. They were so used to watching television commercials that the truth would have just confused them."

"Then what happened, grandpa?"

"The phrase spread everywhere. A governor in California kept switching his story and lying about how he happened to fire a couple of unusual employees. But nobody said he was lying. They said there were serious doubts about his credibility.

"And as the years passed, people forgot about words like liar and lie. It sounded so intellectual to say it the other way. Finally they started getting rid of the old words in books and literature. Now you have to look in an old book like this one to see it.

"Why, it's even taught in the schools. Do you remember what you learned about the cherry tree and George Washington?"

"Sure, grandpa. When his dad asked him who cut that tree down, George Washington said: 'I do not wish to create a credibility gap, Father. I chopped down the tree.' "

"And what do they call Abraham Lincoln in your history book?"

"They call him Creditable Abe."

"When you get to high school, sonny, you'll find they even changed Shakespeare. He used to always be writing about lies and liars."

"Like what?"

"In a play called *Othello*, he wrote: 'You told a lie, an odious damned lie: Upon my soul, a lie, a wicked lie.' "

"Oooh, that sounds exciting, gramps."

"Sure it was. But now Othello says: 'Your credibility is questionable: Upon my soul, a credibility gap, a wicked credibility gap.' "

"I get it, grandpa. It's like when you stop in the tavern and then say you were stuck in traffic and grandma calls you a drunken old credibility gapper."

"You aren't supposed to hear that, sonny ... ."

"And you tell her that there is nothing wrong in telling a little white credibility gap. Is that right?"

"Sonny, ask me no questions and I'll tell you no credibility gaps."

An Automated Accident

Somewhere a computer sneezes or coughs or blinks. That is all it takes today and somebody has problems.

It happened to Miss Cathy Mallon, a Chicago book-keeper, about two years ago. A credit card company abruptly stopped sending monthly bills to her although she owed them money and was using their card.

Miss Mallon sent a letter to the company—American Express—and asked them for her bill so she could pay it.

A form letter came. It said that if she would send along her monthly bill, they would correct her account.

This was the first hint that she was not doing business with a human being. If it was human, it had to be a moron.

She sent another letter, pointing out she could not send her monthly bill because she did not have it. And that was why she was writing in the first place—to get her monthly bill.

An immediate reply: "Send us your bill and we will correct your account."

There is no reasoning with a demented computer. She realized this and did not write again, fearing that it would fly into a rage and come after her.

Instead, she tried phoning the company. "I talked to people and they were nice but they all sounded like machines. I still am not sure if they were really people. They said they would look into it."

This was all in 1965. Last January, she finally got a bill from the company. It was much less than it should have been. But it provided Miss Mallon with a chance to try again to set things straight.

She sent a check for fifty dollars. This was less than she owed, but she hoped that if it was swallowed up by the computer, it might have the effect of getting her account straightened out. This is something like slapping a table radio when it is out of order.

The check was accepted, but the computer or its keeper

did not send her a corrected statement, or any statement at all. Besides being crazy, it was bad mannered.

A couple of weeks ago something finally happened. Miss Mallon got a form letter telling her that her delinquent account had been turned over to a collection agency. Somewhere out there, a mustacheoed computer was preparing to tie Miss Mallon across the railroad tracks.

"I only got the credit card to establish a credit rating in the first place. Now my credit rating is going to be ruined. They should not permit insane machines to do this to people," she said.

An official at American Express' Chicago office said, in a very soothing voice, that he was sorry about what is happening to Miss Mallon and her credit rating.

"When you automate—and we are highly automated— you run into problems. We still have a lot of bugs to iron out and these things happen from time to time.

"We have two million card holders . . . so you have to expect some flaws in the system."

Of course. We must learn to live with computers that turn people over to collection agencies while they are pleading to be permitted to pay their bills.

I suppose someday we will learn to live with even more dramatic computer errors.

It won't be at all surprising when a government computer in Washington hiccups and somebody is erased from the voter lists, Social Security rolls, armed forces records, the FBI files, the census figures, income tax files and everything else.

He will become the man without a number—the twentieth-century version of the man without a country. And he won't have any idea how he got that way.

Kiddie–MACE to the Rescue

It is sad but true that war brings great scientific achievements. Man's creative genius goes into high gear when he seeks a better way to blow someone up.

Wars have led to the development of many of our wonder drugs, synthetic materials, electronic marvels, the nuclear age and new medical techniques.

Now, out of our biggest domestic problem—racial conflict in the cities—there may come something that could be of great use in making day-to-day life more peaceful for millions of Americans.

This occurred to me as I sat in a restaurant the other day and saw a familiar scene unfold.

A young couple and their three small children were having dinner.

From the moment they arrived, the youngest child, about two, was grabbing, throwing and biting everything in sight. He paused only to howl when a knife or something else was pried from his grip.

The two older children, about five and six, kept busy punching each other, crying, pouting, unscrewing salt-shaker tops, stealing the cherries from one another's kiddy cocktails and refusing to eat what they had, or asking to eat what they didn't have.

The young father did what he could, but nothing helped. After two fast martinis, he could still hear them. So he sat there in the classic pose, eyes squinting, teeth gritting, hissing threats of the terrible things he would do when he got them home.

The young mother used one hand to eat and the other to break up fights, replace napkins and get in an occasional soft, but satisfying, slap.

Halfway through the main course, the three began whining, "When are we going home?" just as they had whined earlier about going out.

There was little the couple could do. It is considered

bad form to beat children in a restaurant, although I would not have objected. But it would have just made them howl louder, which wouldn't have solved anything.

And beating them later, as good as it feels, would not undo the damage to the father's digestion and the mother's nervous system.

The answer is to somehow calm the children in the restaurant without breaking dishes or permanently disabling the kids.

Some day there just may be a simple solution to this problem.

The current strife in our cities has resulted in the development of something called MACE.

It is a spray-can chemical used by policemen to subdue people without harming them. A squirt or two in the face and the fight goes out of a man.

Some day, I would hope, a milder form of MACE might be available for domestic use.

If that couple in the restaurant had had a can of child-MACE, one squirt and the three kids would have slumped in their chairs in a pleasant stupor.

It might not have even been necessary. Just the threat —"You be good or mommy will MACE you"—might have been enough.

Restaurants now supply highchairs and kiddy cocktails. Some might provide free child-MACE to couples who forget theirs.

Its uses would go beyond dining out.

At bedtime, when millions of children across the land are screaming and throwing themselves about at the shock of once again having to sleep, millions of MACE cans would bring peace to America's homes.

Parents are never more trapped than when making a long motor trip with children in the back seat. It is not easy to wallop a child while doing sixty-five on a tollroad, although it can be done with practice.

But when they start trying to shove each other out the

windows, or just jump and shout, as they enjoy doing, the driver need only say: "Dear, MACE them a bit and put another tape on the stereo."

Half the population is under twenty-six and it will probably get even worse. If we are to live together in peace, something like child-MACE will be necessary.

And future generations will grow up recalling how mommy sang:

> "Rock-a-by, baby,
> In the tree top,
> Out comes the MACE
> And the tantrum will stop."

They Try Harder

Something I wrote about water and air pollution has hurt the feelings of U.S. Steel Company.

An executive for the company wrote me a letter telling me I don't appreciate how hard they are working, and how much they are spending, to get rid of pollution. And he was nice enough to send copies of the letter to my bosses.

He said that I have done "a great disservice to a lot of hard-working and sincere people, and to a company which has endeavored to operate in every way as a good corporate citizen for the more than sixty years it has been in existence."

His letter makes me feel like a bully for having picked on all these hard-working people and that good corporate citizen. And an elderly citizen, yet.

So I'd like to apologize to U.S. Steel for picking on them.

I had written that U.S. Steel's daily waste discharge into Lake Michigan would fill a bucket the size of the Merchandise Mart.

And I had said that the $200,000,000 it claims to have spent over the last twenty years wasn't enough. If it had been enough, there wouldn't be air and water pollution.

It is clear to me now that my logic was simple minded and that I was being terribly unfair.

You see, I am too dumb to understand high finance. That's why I thought U.S. Steel was getting away with something.

I was under the impression that all businesses operate basically the same way. They sell something, take the money and pay the necessary expenses, and what's left over is profit.

A restaurant owner, for instance, could save money by tossing his garbage into a neighbor's yard, or dumping it in the middle of the street.

But he would get in trouble, so he pays a scavenger service to haul it away. That's part of his overhead.

163

That led me to reason that U.S. Steel should be spending whatever it takes to completely avoid dumping its garbage into my air and into my piece of Lake Michigan. That, I figured, is part of its overhead.

What I didn't realize is that they probably can't afford it and they are doing the best they can.

I thought they had enough dough. But I have since looked over some of their financial statements and now I see that I was asking too much of U.S. Steel.

It is true that they have taken in a pretty good piece of money during the last twenty years. Their sales have been about $70,000,000,000 (pronounced seventy billion dollars).

But that figure is deceiving.

Out of that they have to pay the help. They have to pay for materials. They have to pay the rent and for upkeep of property, and for new property. They have to pay their taxes and Social Security and interest on loans and all the other things that businessmen have to worry about.

And out of that they also spent that $200,000,000— about one-third of 1 per cent of total sales—to do away with their air and water pollution.

By the time they finished, there wasn't too much left over.

For those twenty years, U.S. Steel's clear profit, its take-home, was only $4,700,000,000 (pronounced four billion, seven hundred million dollars).

With that kind of nickel-dime profit, I can see why they've been limited to spending $200,000,000 on eliminating air and water pollution. If they had spent twice as much, their profits would have been murdered. All they would have had left would be $4,500,000,000 (pronounced four billion, five hundred million dollars). And that's not even walking-around money today. The sixty-year-old good corporate citizen might have had patches on its pants.

So I want to say how sorry I am for having implied that

they were cutting corners on air and water pollution in order to show a big profit.

It is clear that they are spending every penny they can afford and are trying their best.

And if we lose a few of the Great Lakes or get a spot or two on our lungs, you can't blame U.S. Steel. Like the old saying goes: You can't get turnip juice out of a turnip.

The California Caper

Here is an exclusive story so big that some people won't believe it.

I got it while having dinner with one of the top TV executives and one of the top movie moguls in the world.

I had long suspected this story existed. So I asked them point blank.

They were so startled they admitted the truth.

In a nutshell, this is it:

There is no such place as California.

It is a mythical state. And all the things that have happened there were just made up.

Once the truth was out, the two men told me the whole story.

How did it all begin, I asked.

"It started innocently enough years ago when Mark Twain wrote something funny about a place he imagined.

"Later, other humor writers realized it was good material and they kept the joke going.

"Then a group of very wealthy men who shared a bizarre sense of humor got together and formed something called 'The Crazy California Caper Club.'

"Their idea was to convince not only the country but the entire world that there was a nutty place called California. And anything fantastic they thought of, they'd say it happened there.

"They controlled the papers, the books and everything else, so it was easier than you'd imagine."

But what happened when people wanted to go to California?

"That was easy, too, and profitable.

"Remember, they controlled the railroads, ships, later the airlines, the highway building companies, the politicians, and they owned land everywhere.

"They'd just run a train or a highway out to some barren place in a swamp or a desert, put up some ranch-style

166

houses, or tri-levels, have a couple of mudslides, forest fires, and then people'd come pouring in."

You mean people who now think they are in California are really . . . ?

"Right. They're scattered all over the world. The town of San Diego, for example, is on the coast of Chile on some land old John P. Rockyfeller wanted to get rid of."

Then their motive was really profit?

"No. Fun was and is the main purpose.

"Those rich old geezers would get together and think of the darndest jokes.

"Like the time one of them said: 'Say, a fellow down at my plant has invented something called a movie camera. Why don't we say there's a place called Hollywood and have movie stars living in mansions, drinking champagne, getting divorced every two days, and make them national heroes.'

"That busted everybody up. They started making up the stars' names—Francis X. Bushman, Rudy Vallee, Rock Hudson, Tab Hunter, Butt Stake. And they went ahead and did it.

"And there was the time one of them thought how funny it would be if people lived in shoe boxes—and out came the idea of the 'California ranch house.'

"And there was the idea of saying there is a parking lot a thousand miles long in California—and the whole concept of expressways was born."

There was the hippies, and the Rose Bowl parade.

"Right. And then somebody thought of making up an Earl Warren. And somebody else thought of having a John Birch Society always going nuts trying to impeach him.

"Actually, it amazed me. We'd just put anything, no matter how wacky it was, on television and say it happened in California, and people believed it.

"Why, I remember the day the club said: 'Hey, let's have a dancer named George Murphy become a U.S. senator from California.' Even I thought that was going too far.

"Well, you know how a joke can snowball. So once we got on the political humor, we stayed with it.

"Yes. I thought of the Ronald Reagan thing. What a party and what a hangover the next morning.

"I guess we went too far, though. What tipped you off —the Ronald Reagan for President gag?"

No. It was the Shirley Temple for Congress bit. Even a hoax must have a touch of believability.

"I told them that would ruin it. I wanted the Little Old Wine Maker to be the candidate."

The Standard Answer

Bill Malloy, a Chicago folk singer, went to Vietnam some time ago to entertain the troops.

After his tour, he traveled to India to fulfill an ambition. He wanted to talk to wise men. And India, as everybody knows, has always been known for its wise men.

Malloy talked to them about the meaning of life. This is the best thing to talk to wise men about, as they aren't much on football and politics.

But when he finished his travels in India and came back to Chicago, he still did not have an answer to the question: "What is the meaning of life?"

One day Malloy noticed the catchy slogan on the Standard Oil service stations' signs: "As you travel, ask us."

He wondered if this might be some kind of omen. If you hang around wise men long enough, you start thinking this way.

So Malloy became a Standard customer, hoping to find what India could not give him.

Every time he pulled into a gas station, he would ask: "As a traveler, could I ask you a question?"

"Yes, sir, that's what our slogan is all about."

"What is the meaning of life?"

The attendants answered in many ways.

One said: "I'm new here."

Another offered: "I don't remember anything in the manual on that."

There was an attendant who said: "I'm not much for church, myself."

And one gave him a leer and a wink, whatever that meant.

Most, however, stared vacantly before cleaning his windshield, even when it was clean, which is meaningless.

Somehow, word of his persistent questioning of attendants got back to Standard Oil's department of customer relations.

And one day Malloy got a phone call at the Inter-University Center, where he works when he isn't singing to folks.

"We understand," the customer relations man said, "that you have been asking our dealers questions and getting unsatisfactory answers."

"That is true."

"What have you asked, may I ask?"

"I have asked them if they can tell me the meaning of life."

"Why do you ask our dealers that?"

"Because your sign says: 'As you travel, ask us.'"

"Well, you must understand that not all of our attendants are trained in metaphysics."

"That may be so; nevertheless you are guilty of misleading advertising because none of them can answer my question."

"We answer most questions."

"Yes, but I am not interested in a good place to eat, a good fishing hole or a clean motel. I want to know the meaning of life."

The customer relations man thought about this for a moment. Then he suggested that Malloy write out his question and send it to Standard Oil with a self-addressed envelope, including his zip code number, of course.

"We will try to find the answer," he promised.

Malloy followed instructions and in a week he received a letter from Standard Oil.

His fellow employees crowded around, but Malloy went into his office and shut the door.

"I wanted to be alone at a time like that," he said.

He opened the envelope. Inside was finally the answer to his question.

It contained an application for a Standard Oil credit card.

Malloy said: "They gave me the only answer they knew."

Cottonpickin'

Economists and educators are worried about the day when most people won't have to work.

Machines will be churning out the things we need. A postal robot will deliver our guaranteed-income checks.

Leisure will become our main activity. Some experts say we'll have to go to college for four years just to learn how to best use our leisure time.

This is going to cause serious problems in planning a vacation. Someday a couple will sit down with their travel folders, resort advertisements and road maps and talk this way:

"John, where are we going this year?"

"I don't know, Mary. I've been so busy at pottery school and moonlighting at the scuba center that I haven't had time to think about it. What's good in those folders?"

"Here's something new. It's a place called the Migrant-Worker-Bleau. They have a package plan. You spend a week picking fruit in California, twelve hours a day. Authentic dirt-floor shack with outside plumbing. Two vitamin-deficient meals a day. Then they supply a 1939 Ford pickup truck, complete with busted radiator and chicken coop on top, and you drive north to pick strawberries for two weeks and live in a shed. The entire deal is $1,255. That's pretty steep but it sounds nice and it's something we could all do."

"That's out, Mary. You know Sally is allergic to strawberries."

"I forgot. Well, here's one for a place in Pennsylvania—the Cave-In-Roc. I'll read the ad: 'Have the vacation of your life! All-round hard labor for the whole family at the finest coal mine resort in the country. Pain-packed 12-hour back-breaking day in the mines for men and boys. Ladies and girls have a choice of waiting on tables in a diner or scrubbing mine owners' homes. Every Friday wildcat strike and fights with company police—FREE! Helmets, picks,

work clothes—FREE! Cave-ins every Wednesday. Two
hundred hovels along railroad tracks. Nearby company
store. $19.95 per day per person (children half-price).'
Doesn't that sound wonderful, John?"

"Oh, I don't know. It sounds just like the Milltown-Bleau.
Boy, was that a gyp. Remember how they advertised a four-
teen-hour work day in the mills and most of the time it
was so crowded we didn't get more than eight hours of
work?"

"Yes, dear. You were so furious you almost came back
home to play golf."

"Well, if I'm going to go all that way just to relax, I
might as well stay home. You couldn't even tell I had been
on vacation. I didn't even get a good stiff neck. You can't
trust some of those ads."

"This one sounds nice, dear, Listen: 'Thirty glorious
sweat-filled days as a railroad hand . . .' Oh, nothing for
the kids to do."

"That's out."

"How about this? 'Have the vacation of your life at the
new, great, sensational Lower East Side Bleau. Hard labor
for everyone in the family. Planned program. Sweatshop
garment factory for the ladies. Pushcart peddling for men.
Choice of shoeshine work or button factory (guaranteed
dangerous machines) for the kiddies. FREE lunch pails.
Stay in a genuine cold-water tenement flat fronting on an
air shaft. (Rooms with hot water $2 less.) Every flat com-
plete with exposed bulbs. Five days and six nights—$22.50
a day (per person). Remember, there is always something
HAPPENING at the Lower East Side Bleau. Our factories
never close!' "

"Gee, Mary, I know how much you like garment work.
But I'm really not that nuts about pushcart peddling. You
get a nice set of calluses, but just once I'd like to come
back from a vacation feeling really exhausted and weak.
That's what a vacation's for, isn't it?"

"Yes, dear, but you know we can't afford to go abroad

and work as pyramid slaves. We just don't have the money this year. Why don't we go back to the good old Cotton-bleau? We always enjoy it, don't we?"

"That's fine with me. I like picking cotton and it's something we can do with the kids. Hey, why don't you call the Cottonbleau right now and ask them if we can get the same tarpaper shack we had last year. Remember—for July. I don't want to miss the sunstroke weather. And tell them we want the sunrise-to-sundown-picking package plan and ask if they still serve the grits and hog jowls . . ."

POLICE WHAT?

Public Enemy No. .98

Sid Marcus is not exactly public enemy No. 1. And for you, not even public enemy No. .98.

His idea of rebelling against society is going through a yellow light at 3 A.M. on a Monday. The sight of a squad car in his rearview mirror makes him sweat for twenty minutes.

Sid is a salesman—full-time, steel products; part-time, ladies stockings wholesale. He sells his merchandise, collects his pay, doesn't cheat, stays out of trouble. He is legit. Therefore society should let him go his own way, right? Wrong.

Not long ago, Sid found out that you cannot stay out of trouble. Today the very act of selling ladies stockings is enough to get you thrown in jail.

Sid was selling his stockings to stores on Roosevelt Road. It was noon and time for him to put a corned beef sandwich and pickle in his stomach.

He drove his station wagon up Roosevelt Road to Western and parked his car near the restaurant on the corner.

This is a tough intersection in a tough West Side neighborhood. If a cop hangs around that corner long enough, he will see people chasing each other for what they have in their pockets.

There was such a policeman hanging around when Sid parked his car. I know the officer's name, but for our purposes he shall be known only as Sherlock.

Sherlock walked over to Sid's car and looked in. He saw the boxes of stockings in the back.

"What's in those boxes? Where are you taking them? Where did you get them?" Stern gaze.

"Ladies' stockings, I'm a salesman, they are samples, I go to stores, I'm going to have lunch." Heavy breathing. Sweat.

Sid rode to the Monroe Street station in the squad car. In the station, Sherlock studied the traffic law book while

Sid sat in a corner. Policemen came and went, glancing at Sid sternly. They always do that. It helps convince a stocking salesman that down deep he is a criminal.

Sid finally cleared his throat and asked: "Is George (Blank) here?" It was the name of a policeman with whom Sid plays handball at the YMCA. He is assigned to Monroe Street.

Sherlock looked at Sid and smiled. "You know George?"

"Sure," exulted Sid, almost tasting the corned beef and pickle now assured him by his influence.

"Good," said Sherlock. "Then I will only give you two tickets instead of four."

"But I didn't do anything wrong," Sid pleaded.

Officer Sherlock then uttered the words that were first spoken centuries ago, when the first act of injustice was committed in some ancient cave:

"Sorry, I've got a job to do."

He wrote two tickets—one for not having a state commercial vehicle license and one for not having the right city vehicle sticker (it wasn't commercial).

Since Sid was carrying samples, his vehicle wasn't any more commercial than, say, an insurance salesman's is because he has blank policies in his briefcase. But this didn't dent Officer Sherlock's determination to meet his ticket quota.

The laws on what constitutes a commercial vehicle aren't crystal clear. But they are clear enough to omit salesmen with samples.

Sid, however, took his tickets and left the station about an hour and a half after he parked to eat lunch.

Worse things could have happened to Sid, and this is not the biggest case of injustice in the city today or yesterday. Maybe it isn't worth this much space in a daily paper.

But a few days ago a horde of punks took over a CTA bus on Western Avenue, not much more than a rock's throw from where Sid Marcus got pinched.

They beat hell out of some of the passengers, took their valuables and got away clean.

They were about as subtle as a linebacker chasing a quarterback.

But Officer Sherlock wasn't around to stop them or catch them. If he was around, he was probably preoccupied looking for Sid Marcus, public enemy No. .98.

Operation Steeple Stop

Chicago police are criticized often enough for not jailing top gangsters. But they seldom get credit for some of their more remarkable achievements.

For instance, few people realize that in recent months the police probably set some sort of record for raiding churches and nabbing ministers.

The official police arrest statistics do not, unfortunately, contain a breakdown of churches and ministers.

But my own official figures show that at least five churches have been raided and at least three ministers pinched.

The most recent raids took place at the Holy Trinity Lutheran Church, 48th and State. This church is said to be directly linked to the Missouri Synod.

There the police grabbed several people in two separate raids, including that church's top man—the Rev. Larry (The Clergyman) Morkert.

Mr. Morkert, who once did a long stretch in a St. Louis seminary, admitted that he has been using the church for more than just preaching sermons and singing hymns.

During the week, he has been opening the place from 11 A.M. to 2 P.M. and has admitted fugitives from nearby DuSable High School. They come there to get "food fixes" —taking bread and meat directly through the mouth.

(Among veteran bread-liners, this is known as main-lining.)

Others come there with, and to read, books passed on to them by book-pushers at DuSable, including several admitted teachers.

The place is also a hangout for volunteer college students who give high school and pre-grammar school students hot tips in such things as reading and math.

Known dropouts and truants have been seen in the church.

Mr. Morkert's alibi was:

"We've been working with these kids, especially the drop-outs and truants, trying to get them to go back and stick with school. We've been successful with quite a few.

"We're also running a pre-school program for small kids and tutoring DuSable students having troubles with studies. They come over during their lunch hours and study periods.

"As far as I can determine, this is simple police harassment. They don't like the fact that we're working in the community, advising people on their rights, giving the young ones a place to go and get together. The commander of the district even told me he thought I shouldn't open the church during the day and that I should boot them out."

The police who raided the church said they found two empty whisky bottles in the women's washroom. An empty wine bottle also was found in the church.

Mr. Morkert said he thinks the police put the whisky bottles in the washroom. But he admitted the wine bottle was his and that he emptied it himself. "In giving communion," he added. He is charged with contributing to the delinquency of minors.

Earlier, there was the hard-hitting raid at the Wellington Congregational Church, 615 W. Wellington. The police nabbed the Rev. James (The Clergyman) Shiflitte, an admitted Presbyterian, for showing a film without a city permit.

And striking on the South Side, the police raided two churches used by ministers working with teen-age gangs.

The police have managed to do all this despite the urgency of their other duties, such as meeting ticket quotas, getting the blue cars washed and making out reports.

They've even pulled in admitted accomplices and associates of the ministers—church and street social workers. And all while handicapped, of course, by Supreme Court rulings that make it difficult to keep a minister in jail once you get him there.

But the police could be even more effective in this important area of law enforcement if a few things were done:

• The police should have a special citywide "Church Squad," just as they have units concentrating on robbery, burglary, traffic, narcotics, public relations and the syndicate. It could quickly strike anywhere in the city when a clergyman is reported stepping out from behind his pulpit and trying to influence teen-age groups, dropouts, the poor and others who are the rightful subjects of the police.

• The public should be asked to co-operate in something like Operation Crime Stop. Maybe it could be called Operation Steeple Stop. Anyone seeing his minister, priest or rabbi—or someone else's, for that matter—up to no good should turn him in to Operation Steeple Stop. Remember, Families That Stay Together, Pray Together—if the preacher makes bond.

• And finally, tougher laws are needed for clergymen. The police must have more effective tools. To begin with, there might be an arena, and maybe some lions. . . .

Shades of Charlie Chan

The vice detectives of the Prairie Avenue police station have won my Police Hero award for August.

They earned it Sunday night by raiding a recreation room in a Chinatown boardinghouse and arresting eighteen Chinese men.

The police said the men were gambling. As proof they gathered in about $20 in change.

This amounts to about $1.11 per Chinese gambler, which would seemingly qualify them for a raid by some anti-poverty agency.

The building that was raided is at 214 W. 22nd Place and the police described it as containing "a Chinese gambling den."

The phrase has a dramatic ring to it. One can almost see a scene in an old movie about San Francisco, with the fog swirling outside and the opium fumes swirling inside, and Boris Karloff made up as Fu Manchu, puffing a water pipe and raking in the winnings.

Most people, however, would say that the building looks like a low-priced boardinghouse. But, then, maybe the Prairie Avenue vice detectives do not see many late movies.

The building is home for a lot of Chinese men, most of them elderly. They live in small furnished rooms.

Like most such buildings—and Chinatown has several —there is one large common room used for reading the papers, watching TV and chatting about how things went with the egg rolls or the starched collars at work that day.

And sometimes they gamble in their recreation rooms. No question about it. It is a sociological fact that the Chinese like to gamble almost as much as they like to shoot off firecrackers. The stakes, though, are seldom big enough to pay for an order of sweet and sour pork.

On Sunday night, I'm told, they were playing something called "restaurant poker." Four men play the game and the others stand around and bet with each other. A Chinese waiter once explained it to me in further detail but that is all I understood.

They did not know that outside several detectives were standing around trying to look Oriental instead of Irish or Polish.

One of them finally put on a disguise—a pair of sunglasses—and came into the recreation room.

It is doubtful that anybody in the room was taken in by the disguise, as half the people in Chinatown know the vice raiders on sight.

The detective later reported that the gamblers talked to each other in Chinese so he did not know what they said. They probably said: "Say, there's that vice detective. Why is he wearing sunglasses? The poor fellow probably has a headache. Somebody get him a nice bowl of won ton soup."

The undercover man finally whipped off his sunglasses and announced that the joint was pinched and his associates moved in.

The big man in the game was said to be Sam (Eggroll) Moy, who is sixty-seven years old. He was charged with running the operation so the others let him sit in a place of honor nearest the door when they rode to the station in the paddy wagon.

One has to go back a long way to find a raid that matches Sunday night's affair. I'd compare it with the night Slats Grobnik and his brother, Fats, were grabbed for pitching pennies on Armitage Avenue. Slats got off when it came out that he was pitching a Canadian penny.

Runner-up for the Police Hero of the Month award was Capt. Martin O'Connell of the Chicago Lawn district.

He is the police captain who achieved some fame by ordering his men to drive street-corner hot dog vendors out of his district.

But that is not why he qualified for the award.

O'Connell, having been successful in his purge of hot dog vendors, put another hard-hitting order in the station's book. He told his men to crack down on peddlers who sell bunches of flowers on street corners, mostly to people on their way to cemeteries or hospitals.

It is not clear why he wants to get rid of men who sell flowers. Maybe he is afraid hippies will buy them and throw them at him.

Snoopers Snooped

The police department is being criticized for planting spies in the peace movement. It should ignore the critics and expand its undercover activities.

As high-ranking police officials have pointed out: The police are simply protecting the "best interests of our society" when they spy on people.

If that's true, then I suggest they infiltrate a very large and important organization—the Chicago Police Department.

Here we have more than ten thousand armed men—and what do we really know about them? Just what they want us to know, really. Just like the peace movement.

Nobody really snoops the police department. So the only time we find out about messy matters is when someone like Jack Muller takes it upon himself to complain.

The police superintendent, or maybe even the mayor, should form a secret super-secret unit to spy on policemen.

It would work something like the police force's super-secret unit that spies on other people. Agents would join the police department. Others would be recruited from within the ranks. They would become trusted by their fellow officers—maybe even become close friends. And they would soak up every little tidbit of information.

Here's an example of the intelligence data they could gather:

An agent, holding a patrolman's rank, is assigned to a squad car with a regular policeman.

After they work together for a few weeks, and the agent wins the trust of the other man, the agent says:

"Christmas is coming, pal, and I'm really short this year. Why don't we make a few dollars from drivers tonight?"

If the policeman agrees, the spy turns in a report for the policeman's secret file. The policeman would never know that such a file exists, so he would never know why his career nose-dived, why he was assigned to pounding a beat near a cemetery. But that is the beauty of a secret-file system: The accused never knows what hit him or why —so one is never bothered with such matters as proof, evidence, etc.

In the peace movement, some police agents assumed minor positions of leadership.

This is a smart move. It could be used in infiltrating the police force.

A spy holding lieutenant's rank could quickly test the honesty of an entire unit—vice, as an example—by telling his men that he wants the area to be "wide open." He would soon know which men were willing to go along and this would be noted in their secret file.

The agents wouldn't be limited to gathering evidence of honesty or dishonesty. By keeping their ears open, agents would soon know how policemen stand politically; if they are loyal to the current superintendent; if they are liberal or conservative; how they feel about minority groups; if they live in the city or, against regulations, in the suburbs; if they drink on duty; if they are faithful to their wives; and so on.

Things like that are always included in secret police files on people. Any personal tidbit can be helpful in assessing a man's loyalty or value. That is what secret files are for.

Word would leak out eventually that the spy system existed. And that would just make it even more effective. Everybody would figure that the next guy is a spy. So they'd protect themselves by turning the next guy in first. Spies would turn in non-spies. Non-spies would inform on non-spies. Spy would be watching spy.

This is the inevitable result of all such spy systems. Not only do the spies gather information, but everybody else becomes an informer. It is very effective in Iron Curtain countries, I'm told.

And when that happens, nobody ever gets away with anything because somebody is always watching and listening. And that somebody is always being watched—by some-body else, who is being watched.

The spy network would be even more effective if every squad car, station washroom and office were bugged with electronic eavesdropping devices. The phones, too. Most policemen believe in electronic eavesdropping, so there wouldn't be many complaints about it.

I'm sure there will be a few policemen who object to a spy network in the department. But that is to be expected. Many reputable, sincere people in the peace movement object to the police spies.

But the protests should be ignored. After all, if a police-man thought someone—such as his best friend—were spy-ing on him, the solution would be simple.

All he would have to do is never say anything. To any-one. About anything. Ever.

That's the whole idea of such a system.

Kids Say the Darndest Things

A kid on the West Side, in the slums, gets two kinds of education. The one he gets in school isn't very good. But the one he gets on the street teaches him things he'll never find in a civics book.

When ghetto kids write essays about how they spent their weekend, there's not much about catching fish with daddy or shopping with mommy. Especially after a weekend of rioting, burning and looting.

Some seventh graders recently wrote about how the riot looked to them, from the inside. They looted, most of them. But they pointed an accusing finger at some surprising accomplices.

Names of the school and the kids have been omitted to protect the teacher's job.

A girl named Sue wrote: "I was on Madison Friday and I saw a lot of people and I say to myself they are fit to riot and they pull down bar and broke window and took clothes from the store and I just look at them.

"Then the police come and the police jump out of the car and got into the window and get something and put it in their car and drove off.

"I got something and ran home . . . and went and got some more. And the third time I went up there I saw the police and I got scare.

"And the police told me to get him some whisky. And I went in a store and got him the whisky and gave it to him and he went and got me some more clothes and gave it to me so I went home and stay there."

Another girl wrote that she happened to be in a store looking for her brother:

"I saw a policeman take two beautiful white and gold lamps out of the window. They had the lamp shades on them. He put them in the back of the squad car on the floor and then start driving again."

Everybody was grabbing stuff at a clothing store, a girl named Sandra writes. She went in.

"The manager at the clothing store took two truck loaded with clothes and told us we could have the rest of the clothes and I was coming out and I saw a color policeman and a white police getting them some clothes. One took a little girls clothes. They took the clothes and put them in the squad car and drove."

Little Charlie wrote a short essay: "When my sister was getting a jacket. She saw a police get a ladys dress. When my sister kept looking at him he said I am taking these to the station."

There was an angry quality to another boy's essay. He had gone out and stolen a TV set and was hauling it home.

"The police stop and come over and take it from me. They put it in the trunk of their car. I was going to take it home and look at it so why did they take it. They should got their own."

And Patricia recalled: "Around my house some of the police did a good job. It was three police in a car, 2 white and 1 color one with 3 TV in the back of the car. And one police told me to go in the store and get him some Seven Crown. And that all I know."

Velma was indignant. "If policemen are stealing or trying to help people to steal, people should go right on and take what they want. Policemen are supposed to be trying to stop people from stealing and not help them to steal."

And Ella tells about this raw deal a kid got:

"The rioting started and the police were looting as much as the Negroes and some more. The police told this boy to put his stuff in the car and they will take him home and for him to ride in the back of the squad car. The police went real fast and the boy fell off and the police kept going with the boy's stuff."

Debby wrote: "When I was walking down Pulaski with my brother we saw a few boys walking with their arms full of clothes. I knew they were new because you could see the tags hanging from them. Then the police came up and took the clothes from them and said: 'Go get your own.' "

Despite what the kids say they saw, police officials say there is little evidence that police were looting.

"Our investigators were told that in some cases shop owners invited police in to help themselves. This, of course, doesn't excuse the officer.

"There have also been reports of instances where shop owners requested police assistance to help remove merchandise from the shops."

So, the police spokesman said: "There's nothing definite. Just complaints and stories."

Those seventh-grade kids do tell some stories.

BY POPULAR DEMAND

Smut—We Love It!

It's unfair to be angry at the Supreme Court for its attitudes on pornography and censorship.

Whether or not the court intends to, it is giving the public what it wants.

There's all sorts of evidence that the mass bookbuyer and filmgoer is looking for vicarious sex kicks and thrills.

And the people who make movies and sell books also are giving them what they want.

At one time, I thought the publishers and producers were shaping the public's tastes, rather than just following them.

But I'm convinced their role is comparable to that of the madam who runs a bordello. She just opens the place, spreads the word, trots out the wares and waits for the customers to show up for what they are interested in.

I'm not talking about the small theaters that carry the sleazy, low-budget "sexploitation" films or the furtive peddler of obvious pornography.

For pornographic kicks—by my fairly liberal standards —you don't have to go beyond the respectable theaters on State Street or the suburban shopping centers.

A recent Frank Sinatra movie, *Tony Rome*, had as crude and obscene a dialog between Sinatra and an old lady as anything I have heard in the Cicero dives.

A Dean Martin film, one of those Matt Helm money-makers, had enough eye-rolling, leering, salivating sex material to satisfy any village idiot.

They aren't "art theater" movies or low-budget "sexploitation" films. They are aimed at the mass, Saturday-night American audience and are shown in the big, respectable theaters and they star two American folk heroes. But the only real difference is that the big theaters have wide screen, so you can see both the head and the feet.

It is likely that the movie *Valley of the Dolls* will be one of the all-time money-makers.

It should be. The critics said it was a lousy, but dirty, movie, based on a lousy, but dirty, book.

Therefore, millions of Americans—salt-of-the-earth Americans—will gallop to the ticket windows with their money in their sweating hands, just as they rushed out to buy the book. If the critics had said the book and the movie were sensitive, meaningful and educational, both would have bombed.

A writer named Alice Payne Hacket has just done a book called *70 Years of Best Sellers.* She lists the top twenty-five best-selling American works of fiction.

The list is proof that what Americans want to read about is usually found at the end of a chapter.

Topping the all-time list is that great titillator of the American housewife—*Peyton Place.* It sold 9,919,785 hard- and soft-covered books.

To show how faithful the titillated American housewife is to her titillating author, *Return to Peyton Place* is the nineteenth highest best-seller, with 4,400,000.

Of the twenty-five all-time best-sellers, fifteen made the list because they were heavy on sex or the authors had reputations for writing such books.

Mickey Spillane, whose hero Mike Hammer solved all problems by shooting someone or flinging them into bed, has seven books on the all-time list, totaling almost 35,-000,000 sales. Show me a pornographer who sells that many over or under the counter.

Erskine Caldwell, whose *God's Little Acre* was the *Peyton Place* of the late forties, has three books on the list. *God's Little Acre* (third) sold 8,065,000. The other two, which sold big because of Caldwell's reputation for bed scenes, totaled almost 9,000,000.

Lady Chatterley's Lover is fifth, with 6,326,000 sales. *The Carpetbaggers* and *Never Love a Stranger*, by Harold Robbins, didn't make the list because of their great messages.

True, the other ten of the twenty-five top-sellers were not

sold on sex impact. But, then, we have to think about other things once in a while.

To illustrate the folly of warning the American public about the dangers of pornography, while the American public is buying it as fast as it can, there is the problem another Chicago columnist has encountered.

He often writes about pornography and how bad things are getting. But he now makes a point of not mentioning objectionable books and movies by name. He has found from experience that this will just send many of his readers charging out to take a look.

Another example of the American's reading taste can be found in the success story of Terry Southern.

He wrote a remarkable book, *The Magic Christian.* The critics praised it. I've never read anything I've enjoyed more. It was brilliant and funny. It didn't sell enough copies to pay the printing bill. It didn't have sex.

He later wrote a book called *Candy.* You remember that one. It was the story of a young girl and her sex adventures. It was meant to be funny, but it wasn't much except dirty. The American public made it a best-seller and it will become a money-making movie.

So be nice to the Supreme Court. If they don't have your best interest in mind, at least they are alert to your primary interest.

Laugh? I Thought I'd Die

Somewhere in the sky, at that moment, a jet plane was crossing this country with Senator Robert Kennedy's body as its cargo.

Down below, a thin young man in a T-shirt hurried through the afternoon crowd on Randolph Street. He took out his wallet as he walked.

He pushed three one-dollar bills at the cashier at the United Artists Theater. As she gave him his ticket and eighty cents change, he glanced at the ad posters.

"Strung up. Whipped. Tortured. McCord gave them 'A minute to pray and a second to' die.' "

He went in the middle aisle but it was crowded, so he went to the next aisle and slid into a seat. He sat low and put his legs up. The movie began and he got what he went there for. Blood, guns, death. Kicks.

There hadn't been enough death, apparently, on his TV screen during the last thirty-six hours. And the terrible black headlines in the papers didn't satisfy him.

None of it was enough for the biggest crowd at any Loop movie-house Thursday—the same day Kennedy died, the day after he was shot in the head.

In the United Artists auditorium, shortly after noon on a work day, there were . . . take a guess: 50? 100? 200?

There were at least 250 people there. Probably 300.

The manager said: "Something like this outdraws anything else downtown."

Why?

"People like the violence. That's the big thing today."

Like most of today's movies, the color is great, the camera work is imaginative. Technically, today's B-movies make yesterday's Academy Award winners look like home-made jobs.

But the technical excellence isn't what draws those crowds.

A few minutes after it began, the hero—a thief and a killer—shot his first man. In the head.

Then he made another man kneel and he put the gun to his head. He smiled and slowly squeezed the trigger. It took a long time and the victim registered terror. The audience laughed.

Get that: the audience laughed. You would have thought it was Abbott and Costello.

The gun clicked. The man gasped with relief that he was not going to have a bullet in his brain. The audience howled.

There was a bigger laugh a few minutes later when two bad guys beat a priest's face bloody with their fists. Then one showed him the contents of a bag—a human head. The priest screamed and ran hysterically to the altar. Laughter. They shot him.

One killer said: "It is bad luck to shoot a priest." Belly laughs.

During the final mass-bloodbath scene, the laughs ran together from one death to another.

A wounded man fell into a fire. Funny. Another lost his gun and the hero kept shooting his feet until he fell backward off a cliff and screamed all the way to the bottom. The laughter drowned out his scream.

After almost two hours, it ended. They came out, swaggering a bit, smiling, gorged with vicarious kicks.

They are easy to describe. They look like the next 300 men you'll see on the city's streets. Black and white, most in casual clothing, some in summer suits. They looked like ordinary American men.

And as they left, others like them were coming in, filling the seats.

It began again. The man knelt and trembled at the thought of a bullet crashing into his brain. And the audience laughed. The priest screamed. The audience laughed.

Outside, people were asking what is wrong with this

country, why it kills the way it does. The world was asking if the United States is that sick and corrupt.

Inside the United Artists, and in theaters across the country, guns were barking, blood was flowing—and people were laughing.

They laughed and laughed. And by then the plane had landed. Now, his family would bury him.

Bonnie 'n' Clyde—the Sad Side

Jim Campbell, a pipe fitter, isn't going to see that movie about Bonnie and Clyde. He knows enough about them already.

He was twenty when the infamous couple came to his part of Oklahoma. The date was April 6, 1934, and Campbell has never forgotten it.

"My father was the constable in Commerce, a small town. The only reason he had the job was because the people liked him. He sure wasn't a professional lawman. He had been a contractor until the Depression, then he lost everything. He was nearly sixty then.

"I was very close to my father. My mother died when I was only three, so my father leaned toward me after that.

"After my mother was gone, he devoted his life to his family, keeping the four kids together.

"That's why he took that police job. It only paid about fifteen dollars a week, but it kept us eating.

"When it happened, I was twenty. I was going to a junior college in the next town. Most of the time I hitchhiked. It was my ambition to be a journalist. You know, you're the first one I ever talked to.

"A farmer came to town that day and told my father some people he passed were in trouble. Their car had gone off the road. My father and another policeman—they were the whole force—drove out there.

"When they stepped from the car, my father was killed instantly. The other man was wounded. I'm sure my father didn't know who killed him. He was just going out to help someone.

"It's ironic. I don't think my father could have shot anyone if he had to. As I said, he got the job because he was well liked and needed it. He really wasn't a policeman.

"I never went back to my classes. I guess I became . . . oh . . . bitter, you might say. I didn't see much point in anything. I just brooded. He had given so much of his life to us, to keeping us a family after my mother was gone.

"I worked in a gas station and did other things like that. Now I'm a pipe fitter (at an atomic energy plant near Kennewick, Washington), a job I enjoy. I probably wouldn't have made a journalist anyway.

"As far as that movie goes, I guess Bonnie and Clyde seem glamorous. The kids are fascinated by them. You can't blame the kids for that, but they shouldn't think they were glamorous.

"They may have had reasons for doing what they did. But they weren't glamorous. Certainly not glamorous."

Russell Moore, a Korean war vet and now a lawyer in Albuquerque, New Mexico, isn't going to the movie. He was less than a year old on Aug. 5, 1932, but he knows about Bonnie and Clyde.

"You're the first person to ever ask me about this. I've wondered if someday somebody wouldn't think to write about this side of it.

"We lived in Atoka, Oklahoma. My father was only thirty-one. My sisters were seven and three.

"My father's family had been wealthy. My grandmother had ranches, farms. But he was a speculator and the Depression wiped them all out.

"My father had us to feed, so he became a deputy sheriff and was glad to get the job.

"It happened this way: My father and the sheriff, Charlie Maxwell, drove up to a dance in Stringtown to look in on things. Their car got stuck in a rut and they walked over to a parked car to ask for a push. The Barrow gang was in the car.

"They gunned my father down with shotguns. They thought he was after them. They wounded the sheriff. He was crippled for life.

"My mother was left with three children to support. We moved in with her parents and she got a job. There was no insurance, but fortunately my father had a burial policy. We couldn't have paid for that.

"My mother was still young and pretty when it happened, but she never married again. She hasn't had a date. Oh, we used to tell her that maybe she . . . well, let's not talk about that now.

"The roughest thing for me was growing up without a father. My grandfather was helpful and understanding. But it isn't the same."

Vernon Humphrey is sixty-two now. He has an auto agency in Alma, Arkansas. But he remembers June 23, 1933, when Bonnie and Clyde showed up near that tiny town.

"I was twenty-eight. The family was just trying to stay alive. We had a farm but you couldn't live off it in those days. I pumped gas at the service station. My father had the city marshal job. He was elected thirty days earlier. It paid fifteen dollars a week. We both worked the farm, too.

"We got a call from another town. Somebody had robbed a store and they wanted my father to block off the road.

"The Barrow gang hit a car in front of them just as my father got there. He and the deputy got out. They got my father with shotguns. He was hit in ten places. He lived for three days and I was with him in the hospital.

"We sold the farm then. I couldn't work it alone. It was hard on my mother. She's in a nursing home now. It was hard on all of us.

"I haven't seen the movie. I couldn't look at it. I don't know if there's anything about my father in it. If there is, I guess it would be what they call a bit part. I hear they made Bonnie and Clyde out to be almost nice people. They weren't nice people."

Claude Harryman farms near Saginaw, Missouri (pop. 189). His father used to farm there until April 13, 1933.

"You know how it was. You couldn't live off the land. My

father was a county constable. No regular salary, just fees for what he did. I was twenty, the oldest of five children. I worked construction and helped on the farm.

"The police from Joplin came into our county. They thought they knew where the gang was. To make it legal, they got a search warrant. But they needed someone from our county to serve it. My father.

"He was on the porch with the paper in his hand when they shot him to pieces. They killed a Joplin policeman.

"We sold the farm. I worked where I could to support the family. For a while I worked in a packing house, butchering animals for $1.50 a day. My mother sewed for the WPA.

"It was a long haul. It wasn't until my brothers and sisters grew up that I could make plans, get married, settle down on my own place.

"See the movie? No. There's nothing in it I'd care to see. I've heard about it."

Many critics say the movie is "realistic." Clyde is handsome, Bonnie is a beauty. They are fun-loving, even cute, dashing and very human. You can sympathize with them. The movie is touching, heartbreaking, brilliant. That's what the critics say. And realistic.

Of course, there's not much in it about the nameless, faceless dead men. Or the orphans and widows and the never-healing scar of a man who never knew his father.

If you put that in, how could you make a movie "realistic"?

Evie 'n' Ade

I'll admit it. I made a mistake about *Bonnie and Clyde*. People who know more about movies than I do have explained my error to me.

I thought that because the real Bonnie and Clyde were vicious killers, it was a distortion of facts to portray them as likable, attractive, sympathetic; to make national heroes out of them. I was wrong.

Knowledgeable people say the movie should be viewed solely as an art form, as entertainment. If it strays historically, that isn't important. History has a purpose. Art has another.

That means there was no point in my interviewing the four men whose fathers were rather callously murdered by the real Bonnie Parker and Clyde Barrow.

If that's what the experts say, I won't argue. In fact, I'll go beyond admitting I'm wrong: I'm going to suggest a plot for another movie.

It will be called *Evie and Ade*.

The movie opens by showing a railroad car standing in the countryside. Inside are men in uniforms sitting around a table and looking glum. There is zither music in the background.

The train door opens and in walks a good-looking young man, wearing a mustache, with a pretty blond on his arm. He smiles and says:

"Hi, I'm Ade Hitler and this is Evie Braun. We take over countries."

Everybody signs surrender papers. Then Evie and Ade jump in a big touring car with Ade's fat buddy, Herman, his skinny buddy, Heinrich, and their wives, and they start back toward Berlin.

There's good-natured ribbing among them about Ade's mustache, Herman's eating too much, etc.

Ade becomes serious when Evie says: "*Liebschen,* honey, this is a big day for you. I bet it will be in all the papers—

and the history books, too. It's not everybody who can take over France."

Ade grows pensive. At this point we use flashbacks to show his early years.

The car scene fades and we see a little boy walking in a little Austrian town. We know he is Ade because even as a child he had a small mustache.

He enters a house and hands his report card to his father, a husky man with a big mustache. The father shouts: "*Dumkopf*, you flunked everything—even mechanical drawing."

The little boy trembles. "But, Father, I passed art. And you know I want to be an artist."

The father hits him with a beer stein. The mother enters and says: "Papa, why don't you leave the child alone. You always pick on him. He will grow up with deep-rooted psychological difficulties."

"*Nein*," the father shouts. "I just want him to study hard so he can be a good paper-hanger."

"Never," the boy cries as he locks himself in his room and draws pictures of his father hanging by the neck.

A few fast scene-shifts follow: A slightly older and sadder Ade at his mother's funeral. Then being turned away by an art school. "You ought to be a paper-hanger," the man says. Ade being wounded and decorated in World War I. Then shuffling along with other unemployed men in the post-war depression. Ade making fiery speeches to hungry men, getting tossed in jail, writing a book in jail.

Then back to the touring car where we opened.

They get to Ade's mountain retreat. Evie and the other wives start dinner, and Heinrich runs out for the papers.

Ade phones someone and says: "I think we ought to try England. But remember, don't drop bombs on any innocent civilians. I'm just after the generals. Good-by."

Heinrich returns with the papers and looks pleased. "You're in the headlines, Ade."

But Ade frowns: "I wish the doctors would do something about the Semitic flu epidemic. Look, the newspaper says another 50,000 Jews have died of it. Some of my best friends, too. And I'll bet the other side tries to blame me for it. Nuttiest flu bug I ever heard of."

Evie pulls Ade's arm: "Forget your problems, *liebschen*, honey, come on to bed."

Ade blushes: "Not until we are married. I've told you that."

Evie pouts: "But when are we getting married?"

Ade: "When I can give you a decent wedding present —the world."

Evie: "I'd just like to settle down in a little white house."

Ade: "Some day we'll settle down in a big White House."

The group laughs. As the scene fades, they relax for an evening of Wagner records, beer and pinochle.

Several vivid war scenes follow. They are intended to let the audience know that when people are shot, they bleed and die. There's some buzz-bombing of London, a Russian winter, a nuclear blast or two, Ade having some of his own generals shot, and so on. Then . . .

Evie and Ade and their pals are in an underground apartment. They are glum. Fat Herm hangs up a phone and says: "We've had it, Ade. They're closing in on us from all sides."

Ade frowns: "Never mind that, What about the flu epidemic?"

Herm: "Still no cure. Some of my best friends . . ."

Evie bursts in with a minister. "Ade, you promised."

They embrace. The wedding is held. They embrace again. The scene fades.

It's the next morning. Evie and Ade and friends are talking over breakfast.

Ade: "You'll like South America, Martin. Good weather."

Evie: "Ade, *liebschen*, honey, I wish you'd change your mind."

Ade: "No, Evie. I've decided. I'll give myself up to the Americans, serve my time and we'll start over again. Gee, maybe I can even go to art school . . ."

They embrace.

The scene shifts. Ade and Evie emerge from the bunker. They see some Allied troops. They wave. Ade yells: "Hi, I'm Ade Hitler, this is Evie Braun. We . . ." Gunshots. Evie and Ade fall, riddled with 42,361 bullets.

As it ends, with zither music playing, we realize that Evie and Ade, like Bonnie and Clyde, were just people like the rest of us, and it hurts a little when they get shot.

My original script called for 9,000,000 bit players, but they won't be needed. It would just confuse the plot.

If the movie is made, some interesting fashions will emerge. I wonder how teen-agers will look wearing little black mustaches and doing a new dance called "The Goose-step"?

That Was the Life

Many of Dr. Richard Kimble's fans wonder how he is doing, now that he is no longer "The Fugitive" and is back home in Indiana practicing medicine.

I took a drive down to Stafford, Indiana, where he lived before being wrongfully convicted of murdering his wife and going on the lam for four years.

He was mowing the lawn in front of his large, tree-shaded house when I arrived. He consented to an interview.

"You don't mind if I keep mowing the lawn while we talk, do you?" he asked.

Not at all, doctor.

"We've got a dinner date at the country club and she'll blow her stack if I don't finish the lawn."

She?

"My wife. You remember her—Jean Carlisle, the girl who helped me right at the end."

I remember. How is she?

"Getting a bit plump."

Well, doctor, how do you like being free?

"Who's free?"

You are.

"Listen, I got this house to pay for, two cars, an expensive country club membership. I spend my days listening to hypochondriacs and my evenings attending civic meetings, medical association meetings, neighborhood improvement meetings. You call that being free?"

What I meant was, you are no longer a fugitive.

"That's right. Now I'm a prisoner. Just between you and me, I sure miss being a fugitive."

You can't be serious.

"Like heck I'm not. That was the life, moving from town to town, working as a bartender, truck driver, laborer, foot loose and fancy free, never paying income tax. I went everywhere and saw everything. Now I'm stuck in this hick town."

Doctor Kimble, I'm shocked . . .

"And the women. Boy, there was always some good-looking woman falling for me when I was the fugitive. It must have been the hunted look in my eyes. I guess women are attracted by that."

Possibly, but . . .

"It might have been my dark hair, too. I had an excuse to dye it then, but now I don't. Be honest—doesn't the white hair make me look a lot older?"

Mmmmm. A bit, yes . . .

"And look at my waist, I'm getting fat."

Oh, a few pounds, maybe . . .

"When I was the fugitive, I was really in shape. Hard as a rock. Lean. Because I was always working hard, hiking on the road, getting in fights, jumping out of windows."

But now you are a doctor, a physician.

"I'd rather be a young, adventurous fugitive than a fat, old doctor."

Nevertheless, you had the satisfaction of catching the one-armed man.

"That was my mistake. If I hadn't got such a complex about him and just forgot about it, I'd still be at large. Those bungling cops would never have caught me."

But the one-armed man killed your wife.

"So? Six more months with her and I'd have done it myself."

But he was an evil, crude man.

"Hah! You should see the crowd at the country club."

Isn't it a relief not to have Lieutenant Girard constantly trying to catch you?

"Lieutenant Girard couldn't catch the flu."

Do you ever see him?

"Sure. They busted him for wasting four years and all that money chasing me instead of the one-armed man. Now he's a traffic cop. He's always stopping me, but I slip him a fin and he let's me go. That's the only thing I enjoy."

But isn't it good to be reunited with your sister, your brother-in-law, your . . .

"My brother-in-law is a boob. They came over last night and he got drunk and spilled a drink all over the sofa. Frankly, I wish he'd been the killer, instead of the one-armed man."

Isn't peace of mind important to you?

"Who has it? Before, all I worried about was a few cops and brushing off some girl who fell for me. Now I read the papers and look at TV and I worry about Vietnam, air pollution and college campus riots."

But you have a wife again.

"All she does is remind me of how she helped me. She'll never let me forget that, boy."

But isn't there some happiness in your life—something to look forward to?

"Oh, sure."

What?

"Another one-armed man."

Cassius Needs Class

Cassius Clay has many personality flaws—arrogance, ignorance, bigotry and a hysterical sort of vanity.

But his most serious problem, the one that gets him in the deepest trouble, is his simple-minded honesty.

He says whatever pops into his uncluttered head. And this is almost unthinkable in the world of sports, where the great stars have learned to talk in a wonderful language that says nothing.

Every time he does it, Clay shocks all the fight experts, who aren't accustomed to this kind of talk.

Monday night's fight, which I watched, was a perfect example.

For weeks, the experts said Ernie Terrell was a bum and Clay was a wonderful fighter and he would beat the daylights out of Terrell.

That is just what happened. It was obvious to everyone who watched the fight that Terrell was, in the language of the fight game, a bum. A brave bum, a likable bum, a bum who could stand around for an hour and be hit on the head and not fall down. But a bum.

When the fight ended, Clay said that Terrell was a bum. And that he, Clay, is the greatest. Everybody got mad at him.

Another thing that upset the experts was the way Clay acted when the fight ended.

There is a wonderful old tradition in boxing.

After you spend the evening punching another man a few hundred times, cutting his face open and trying to knock his head into the balcony, you are supposed to hug him like a long lost relative from the old country.

Clay didn't do this. He acted like Terrell was someone he had been in a fist fight with and didn't particularly like.

So, once again, many of the experts are bemoaning the great tragedy of Cassius Clay.

This tragedy, as they explain it, is that he could be a beloved, idolized, confetti-parade champion.

The experts say he could even be one of the most popular champions "of all time," which covers quite a few years.

All he has to do, they have explained, is be a nice guy —show some class.

Translated, this means that he should stop saying what he thinks.

The experts are right. Cassius could be a popular fellow right now if only something like this had happened Monday night:

"Cassius, you won almost every round and beat him to a pulp. Was this one of your easiest fights?"

"Gosh, no, Jack. This was a very tough fight. Ernie is a very tough boy and a fine fighter. I was just lucky to be in good shape and to land a few good blows."

"Did he hurt you at any point in the fight?"

"*Did* he! Ow! I still hurt.

"He landed a lot of good blows. He's a very tough boy. I was just lucky to be in good shape and to have a wonderful mother who had faith in me and fed me good, nourishing food. Hi, Mom. Can I wave to my mom?"

"Sure Cassius. Now, did he . . ."

"Can I wave to your mom?"

"Sure, but . . ."

"Hi, Jack's mom. You're lucky, Jack, to have such a wonderful mom. She's in wonderful shape and so are you, Jack."

"Thanks, Cassius. But about the fight. You said earlier that you were the greatest. Are you convinced of that now that you've beaten Terrell?"

"Aw, gee, Jack, I'm really not that great. I was just talking silly. Actually, I'm lucky to be here, thanks to the wonderful fans, the wonderful people out there in TV land, you, your mom, Ernie, who is a very tough, fine fighter, everybody's mom, Abe Lincoln, General MacArthur, the

President, J. Edgar Hoover, Abe Lincoln's mom, all the fans' moms. . . ."

"Was it a close fight?"

"Close? I thought Terrell won. Honestly. He's a tough, determined boy. So, *he's* the greatest."

"But the judges gave you almost every round."

"They are wonderful guys and I appreciate their generosity and the generosity of the fans, and your generosity, Jack, and . . ."

"But it looked like he didn't even hit you."

"Well, you know more about those things than I do, Jack, you and the other experts, but believe me, I'm *lucky* to be alive. He's a wonderful boy. I want to hug him again, now that he's stopped bleeding and is on his feet. . . ."

"Just a second, Cassius, one more question. What are your plans for the future? Who will you fight?"

"There are so many worthy contenders, Jack, that it is hard to say. Ernie deserves another shot at it, and he'll probably win, and Patterson and John L. Sullivan . . ."

"Sullivan is dead."

"Oh, I'm sorry to hear that, Jack, he was a wonderful guy and so are you."

"Please, don't hug me, Cassius."

"Sorry."

"Before we let you go, I'd like to say that you are a wonderful champ and a swell guy."

"Jack, hearing *you* say it is the most important thing in the world."

"That's the way it should be, champ."

The Un-American Sport

One of the most un-American business operations in America is major league baseball, the great American pastime.

A baseball player can't work for the team of his choice. If he tries to quit his job with one team and play for another one, he is pushed out of the game altogether.

A man who wants to start a major league baseball team can't do it without the permission of the other men in the same business.

When not stifling the free enterprise of the players or the people who want to start teams, the baseball owners show that they haven't got any initiative of their own by always trying to mooch free stadiums from the taxpayers.

Despite these flaws, I have always been a baseball fan.

Who can be critical of baseball once the game starts, the excitement mounts and the manager comes out of the dugout and talks to the pitcher, scratches his head, rubs the ground with his toe, gazes at the bullpen, waves his arm, slaps the departing pitcher on his backside, slaps the incoming pitcher on his backside, talks to the catcher, whispers to the third baseman, nods at the umpire and waddles back to the dugout.

But now, baseball has gone too far. Maybe it is time Congress investigates the way it treats employees. Maybe the Teamsters should come in and organize a ballplayers' union.

I am talking about the thing that happened to Bo Belinsky, a pitcher for the Houston team and one of the finest sporting-world figures since Errol Flynn. What his employers did to him would cause a strike if he worked in a factory.

Belinsky was in Florida, which is where many teams go to practice and exercise before returning to their home cities to sit in the dugouts in earnest.

Last Saturday evening he phoned the manager or some other boss with a request.

I don't know the specifics of the conversation, but it

seems Belinsky was on a date with a young lady whose picture once appeared in *Playboy* magazine.

Apparently they wanted to watch the late-late movie or something, and he said he would like permission to return to the camp at 3 A.M. instead of midnight, which is the team's curfew.

This doesn't seem like an unreasonable request. Very often the best movies—*Godzilla* or *Charlie Chan*—don't come on until midnight.

But the manager said no. He ordered Belinsky to say good night to the girl and return to camp. This angered Belinsky, which is understandable, because anybody knows that watching *Godzilla* by herself could give a young girl nightmares.

Besides, Belinsky wasn't sleepy. If he were sleepy, logic tells us, he would not have to be told to come back to camp. And since he wasn't sleepy, why should he lie awake listening to other baseball players snore? This would probably make him so nervous he wouldn't be able to slouch on the bench properly the following afternoon, or even rub the shine off a ball.

So Belinsky got angry and refused to come back at midnight. He packed up and left the baseball camp and hasn't come back. Nobody knows where he went. Probably to some place where a thirty-year-old man is free to watch the late show in peace.

As a sports fan, I consider it a personal loss. There are a lot of athletes who try to set an example for children. But there aren't many who can be heroes of my generation.